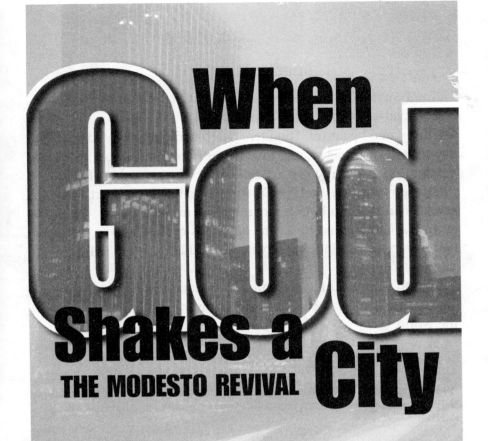

When God Shakes a City

THE MODESTO REVIVAL

glen berteau

with joel kilpatrick

foreword by rich wilkerson

Gospel Publishing House
Springfield, Missouri
02-0838

Special Thanks

To my wife, Debbie, who has the greatest passion for prayer and revival of anyone I know in the world

To my two beautiful daughters, Kelli and Christy, who have supported, encouraged, and loved me through many ministry challenges, and to my son, Micah Glen, who is my best friend

To the ministerial staff at Calvary Temple whose heart for revival continues to birth a move of God in our City

To our Church family for the hundreds of hours given in dedication to working the harvest while the fields are still white

And to Rudy and Karen Krulik, founders of Reality Outreach, for their friendship and vision for lost souls around the world

---

All Scripture quotations are taken from the New King James Version. Copyright © 1997, 1980, 1982 by Thomas Nelson, Inc. Used by permission. All rights reserved.

Library of Congress Catalog Card Number 97-72579
International Standard Book Number 0-88243-838-7

Printed in the United States of America

Contents

Foreword

I first met Glen Berteau in 1978. At the time, both of us were involved in youth ministry. He ministered in Texas, and I in California. Glen spent a week in our home, and it was at that time that I first learned of his great passion for leading people to Christ.

If I have ever met someone who lives the definition of "evangelist" in life and ministry more than Glen Berteau, then surely I have forgotten that person. In fact, I have known some pastors who try to evangelize and some evangelists who try to pastor, each with varying degrees of success. Glen Berteau thrives in both arenas.

From the first time we met, I watched Glen grow to national prominence in youth ministry. Through a tragedy beyond his control, Glen was forced to leave the field of youth ministry and pioneer a new church. For five years, that church grew.

One day Glen called me and said, "Rich, I have just been called to move to Modesto, California, to become senior pastor of Calvary Temple!" Calvary Temple was a church I knew well, having served as youth pastor just north of there in Sacramento during the 1970s.

Calvary was like many historic churches in the United States and Canada: It was at a crossroads. Some members wanted to maintain the heritage of the church. Other members desired a fresh move of God and a revelation of Jesus for their generation.

Contemporary pastors who assume the leadership of these third- and fourth-generation churches must steer through many obstacles as they take them to new levels of ministry. This was the case at Calvary Temple in Modesto when Pastor Berteau took the helm of that great church. He did so with a keen awareness that without divine intervention and the miracle-working power of God, the church would get stuck in the routine of "doing church."

But God intervened! He shook Modesto out of complacency and in three years brought sixty thousand people to that altar in one of California's greatest revivals. What happened in Modesto reads like a page from the Book of Acts. As church after church experiences awakening in this age of revival, many can look back to the Modesto revival as the harbinger of things to come. It was one of the first—perhaps the first—great revivals of the 1990s.

Should Jesus tarry, this generation will see the end of one millennium and the beginning of another. Someone once said, "Change is inevitable." But the Modesto revival only emphasizes that Jesus Christ is the same yesterday, today, and forever.

—RICH WILKERSON
Evangelist

Chapter 1

The
Shaking Begins

*A*s I drove down Coffee Road and watched the rain pour down onto my windshield, my wipers could hardly keep up with the torrents of water. We were experiencing the worst rainstorms California had seen in twenty years. I could just see the red blur of brake lights in front of me. Already a gloomy darkness was falling on Modesto, even though it was only half past five on a cold and drenched Sunday evening.

I was on my way to the church for prayer before our evening service. But that night was not supposed to be an ordinary service. It was the first night of a three-night drama we were hosting called "Heaven's Gates & Hell's Flames," sponsored by Reality Outreach in St. Catherines, Ontario, Canada. We had chosen this powerful presentation as a major outreach tool to reach the city of Modesto, and the church had gotten behind it with their whole hearts. But things were not looking so good as I drove toward the church, guiding my car carefully through the traffic. As I was getting closer and closer, I feared the evening to be a monumental failure.

We had needed a new parking lot for a long time, but the asphalt had not been laid in time for the drama presentation because of the storms, and now half the parking lot was nothing more than mud and mire, a virtual minibus bog. If more than our usual number of people came that night, they wouldn't have any place to park, and our attendance would be limited.

That was weighing on my mind.

And the rainstorms . . . what could I say about them? We had prayed and hoped for good weather to attend our opening night, but those hopes were out the window by the time the second week of heavy rains came pounding in from the Pacific.

We had wanted to draw hundreds, maybe thousands, of unbelievers to the drama so that they could understand the reality of heaven and hell and of Jesus Christ's saving power, but now it was a matter of getting the church members themselves to come out, let alone the rest of the community.

That was also weighing on my mind.

As I drove along thinking and praying, it seemed that nothing had been conducive to the drama's success, and I was sure I would go down in Modesto history as the man who manufactured the city's biggest blunder. Our church would look silly to the rest of the community, the people in the church would lose faith in our vision, and any further attempts at outreach would suffer. In other words, everything I had been working toward would fall like a house on stilts, and the people would walk away discouraged and disappointed, not just with me or Calvary Temple, but with God.

I shouldn't have felt downcast, but part of me—a big part—did. I knew our church was ready to evangelize the community in a visible way, identifying ourselves with the gospel. And yet as we were making our first moves, we were about to stumble.

By now I was downright depressed.

As I came within a few blocks of the church, I began to notice something strange. People were huddling under umbrellas and walking in the same direction I was driving. Cars were parking in grocery store lots that should have been empty on a Sunday night. People were getting out of their vehicles in the pouring rain, jerking their coats over their heads, running down the sidewalks, splashing water on one another, and soaking pant cuffs and dress hems.

I wondered for a split second if there were not some sort of big event in town that I had not heard about, maybe a concert or emergency food and shelter. Perhaps a levee had broken and the town was running for higher ground (it hadn't happened for many years, but anything seemed possible with this rain). But the closer I got to the church, the more huddled groups of soaked and bedraggled people I saw walking alongside the road—not only that, but they seemed animated and excited. Some of them were even dressed up nicely. I saw more and more people wading through the puddles and thought to myself, *They are all determined to get somewhere, but where in the world are they going?*

The church parking lot at Calvary Temple Assembly of God told the tale as I pulled in and saw hundreds of cars filling the spaces. Bumper to bumper and crammed in next to one another, many of them parked haphazardly and in all sorts of crazy ways so they wouldn't have to park elsewhere and walk long distances. Our church parking lot, which I had expected to be empty, was a multicolored checkerboard of rain-spattered car roofs.

It looked like halftime at the Super Bowl.

People were not walking in the rain for a concert; they were not walking half a mile for emergency shelter; the levees had not broken; no circus was in town. These people were walking through the rain to see our church's production of "Heaven's Gates & Hell's Flames"; they were coming to hear about God's saving grace, the real emergency need in their lives.

Incredible though it seemed, I had to believe what I was seeing. I

9

began to pray, "Oh, Lord Jesus, I don't know what's happening here, but, God, I ask You to bless these people for coming out tonight. Lord, just bless them." As I nosed through the parking lot looking for a space—a space in my own church—I was amazed by the number of people streaming into the sanctuary. It was only half past five, the time when the ministers and elders come in half an hour before the service to pray, the time when the sanctuary is dotted with just a few devoted prayer warriors kneeling at the pew.

I got out of the car and joined the lines of people walking toward the sanctuary. When I went inside, people had already filled the pews, dripping wet but happy and animated. As the six o'clock hour approached, the streams of people had become rivers flooding through our doors. The first arrivals were forced to scoot in close to one another to make way for the constant inflow of people—adults, children, teenagers, men, women, families, singles. I had never seen a better cross section of the community. The sanctuary was buzzing with excitement and was full not just of people but of a palpable, spiritual energy that seemed ready to burst through the walls. Before the production had even started, the Spirit was resident among us, preparing our hearts, setting the tone, establishing His presence so that lives could be radically changed.

The twenty-five-hundred-seat sanctuary was full, and we were forced to turn away over one thousand people, asking them to come back for the Monday night performance. The rain had not dampened the spirits of people in Modesto as I had expected it to. If anything, it had brought our dry community back to life.

God himself had come to Modesto.

When I got home that night I was still numb—from the wind and rain, yes, but also from the unprecedented response to the drama. Not only had people come to see "Heaven's Gates and Hell's Flames," but the impact on our visitors had been enormous, and when we gave the altar call people flooded the stage. Not just forty or fifty people responded, which would have been a normal response; not just three hundred or four hundred, which would have been a phenomenal

10

response. No, that night more than eight hundred people came forward and gave their lives to the Lord.

"Debbie," I said to my wife as we were getting ready to sleep, "we're in the midst of a great work, and God is doing something that we don't have any control over. It's not just a good meeting down at Calvary Temple or some evangelist getting the church people excited—God is doing something way beyond our efforts."

It was then that I knew that the time had come for Debbie and me to see a city won for God. Not just part of a city, not just one corner of it, not just this community or that community, not just this group of people over here and that group over there, but the entire city. It was going to be a wholesale victory for the Lord, a no-holds-barred invasion of hell, a last-call, come-as-you-are party where the whole town turned out to celebrate Christ their Savior—the kind of celebration we had prayed for and dreamed about for so many years.

Chapter 2

"Boom-Boom" Berteau

*Y*ou need to get saved, Glen Berteau!"

"Shut your mouth, Denny Duron!"

How many times had the people on the Louisiana Tech campus in Ruston, Louisiana, heard that? Probably a thousand or more. It was almost our little script, and we performed it over and over for nearly three years.

Denny and I were both on the football team and as sports stars we received more than our fair share of attention. But though we shared the same goal on the field, off the field we were heading in two totally different directions; in fact, in spiritual terms, we were hardly even playing the same game.

I was not much of a sports star during most of my high school years. I was like most of the other youth who tried out for football, basketball, and track, with one major exception: I was much smaller than they were, and my only natural asset was speed. Nevertheless, I played football for three years in a nondescript manner as a defensive back. I was not a bad player, but I didn't stand out.

In my senior year, however, the coaches changed their minds and decided to put me at running back. Now, as a short guy with not too much muscle or bulk, I was scared to death of the eleven other players on the field who wanted to kill me. You might even say that I was blessed with an overwhelming spirit of fear, and fear can do a lot of things to a young person.

In my case, it made me faster. I was timed in the forty-yard dash at four and a half seconds.

Up to that point, not many people had heard of me. I had started on defense—an above average ballplayer—but not on offense. After our first couple of games, though, everyone suddenly realized that Glen Berteau could run fast, that he could score touchdowns. I ran around the defensive line, or through the defensive line, any which way to avoid getting crushed by the other guys, who were twice my size and whose goal was, of course, to kill me. Few people could catch me once I had broken into a dead run, and suddenly the team began depending on me: I was the go-to guy on offense. The crowd cheered every time I broke away, and their cries for victory fueled my speed. I loved the contact of the pads, the hitting, and the crowd, when at times seventeen thousand people watched us play.

Our high school team was the Broadmore Buccaneers, and we had a big ship's cannon that went off every time we scored a touchdown. It was filled with all sorts of junk—paper and confetti and streamers—and made a loud boom when they set it off. It rattled the windows on nearby houses, and we hoped it rattled the opposing team too. At the time, I was averaging two touchdowns a game, which meant the cannon went off twice every game: "Boom! Boom!" Everyone loves a nickname, and the local newspaper picked up on this. Every week they would write the headline: "Boom-Boom Berteau Leads the Bucs to Another Victory." Hence the nickname I carried from high school all through college.

13

I had been named all-city, all-state, all-Southern, all-league, and all-American as a high school running back. Because of that outstanding season, I got a lot of attention from college football coaches. A year before, no one had ever heard of me; now I was getting calls from all over the country. The late "Bear" Bryant had watched me play and wanted me to attend his school. All sorts of coaches from the major southern universities were trying to recruit me, and many offered me a full scholarship. They wanted to pay for my tuition, my books, my food, my housing, everything. This was an amazing development for me and my family because my father had lost his job a year earlier and wouldn't have been able to put me through school.

By this time I had become obsessed with football and had developed the mind of a football player. I was mentally tough, a winner at heart, and my life was the game. My only goals lay between the grid lines. I thought the ultimate achievement was setting foot in the opponents' end zone and rubbing the score in their faces.

As a true sports convert, I adopted *Sports Illustrated* as my Bible. One issue came out with Terry Bradshaw on the cover, the blond bomber from Louisiana Tech University, the number one draft pick of the Pittsburgh Steelers, and I was in awe. He was a Louisiana boy and the number one pick of the Steelers! I showed the magazine to my dad one afternoon, and while we were standing there ogling it the phone rang.

"Hello, is Boom-Boom there?"

"This is Boom-Boom."

"This is Terry Bradshaw. I hear you are a pretty good football player."

I motioned wildly for my dad to come over.

"Well, I'd like you to come up and visit Louisiana Tech and play football for us on a full scholarship," he said. "Would you think about it?"

Not only did I think about it, I did it. It took only one visit and one meeting with Terry Bradshaw to convince me, and that is how I became an all-conference running back at Louisiana Tech, winning two national championships. That was the road I decided I wanted to take, the life I wanted to lead, and since I have always had a radical, all-or-nothing personality, I went into it with my whole heart.

But I was missing the main goal in life. I had all the respect in the world for football coaches, but no regard for God, the "Coach" and Creator of the universe (including the gridiron). Like most young men I was brash, overconfident, and in need of nothing but an admiring crowd.

Chapter 3

Dying in Martinez

y 1984, twenty-two-year-old Tammy Jones had all but given up on life. The brown-haired woman with a sweet and level voice had tried death too many times to count. But she couldn't even do that right, let alone face the life that had been handed to her in a garbage pail.

Beyond hopelessness, beyond desperation, her mind addled by drugs, Tammy wandered listlessly through the corridors of her boyfriend's house. To him it was a home; to her, it was a jail cell. The walls of her bedroom may as well have been solid metal bars, and the gated yard a Cyclone fence with razor wire. She didn't even own her own body, her feelings, her emotions. Every aspect of her being had been auctioned off at a young age without her permission, without her choice, given away to strangers for their various perversions and pleasures. As for getting out of the situation, that was always easier said than done, especially when she depended on her boyfriend for nearly everything, even loving his cruelty because he fulfilled her desire for acceptance, attention, and love. For years it had been that way, not just years but lifetimes, repeated over and over in the mind of a little girl, then an adolescent, and now a young woman. The thorns of the past had intertwined themselves into the very fiber of her personality; who she had wanted to be never mattered, not to anyone else and not to herself. No, Tammy wasn't going anywhere.

She had tried before.

When she was a teenager the situation at her mother's house had become so rancorous that she tried to flee, taking buses, cars, whatever took the most direct route out of Martinez, California. Though the freedom of the road offered temporary exhilaration—the fresh air, the unknown places—ultimately, it didn't, and couldn't, amount to anything. Her past was a magnet drawing her inevitably back to itself, the loathsome sun around which she orbited, never breaking free.

One time she had gotten well away from the hellish streets of Martinez to Oklahoma, the prairie land where she thought that maybe, just maybe, she could plant the seeds of a decent present and reap a brighter future. But the father of her children destroyed the dream when he followed her by the same road she had taken and brought her back to Martinez, a devastating homecoming for the queen of losers, for that was how Tammy thought of herself.

Escape was always on her mind: the right time to leave, the right road to take, the right door to sneak out of, the right things to take and clothes to wear. But where was the map that would tell her the road out of her misery? Which avenue, which street, which back alley would glimmer in the moonlight, beckoning her to a new place where the old could be forgotten and where the dreams of a little girl could be reborn in the heart of a jaded and abused young woman? The map didn't exist, not for Tammy Jones, and when she tried to escape— over and over again, like a recurring nightmare, she was always found out, always discovered. Worst of all, her own weakness complied with the wishes of those who wanted to steal her back. She was so dependent on the man who had taken over her life and so confused and dazed by drugs and the pressures of taking care of two children (children she had not intended, children she had not prepared for), that she was unable to make a permanent break. For his part, the man bred insecurities in her, perverting the words of the Bible and convincing her that she was possessed by the devil, which meant that he was her savior, which meant that she owed him everything.

Tammy Jones was born to an alcoholic mother in Berkeley, California, in 1962. Her father—a shadow figure, known better by other women than his own family—abandoned the family when she was just a baby. Tammy grew up under the supervision of a woman who smelled not like freshly baked bread or clean clothes, but like vodka and wine, a woman whose only real concern was where—and how—she could get her next drink. To call her Mother was to affirm the biological fact, but beg the emotional question: When someone loves the bottle more than her own child, does *Mother* really mean anything? Where does the child go when she hurts? Into the drunken arms of a barstool maven? Tammy saw the door close on the most precious relationship a little girl could have. When she sought comfort in her mother's bosom, alcohol on her breath undermined any words she might say.

Mom would take Tammy to the local bars, stumbling down the street, desperate for a drink and with a four-year-old girl in tow. Wide-eyed and innocent, Tammy went along. The legs of the barstools became her jungle gym; underneath the tables, her hideouts; the legs of patrons, her playmates in the world of make-believe. The bars became Tammy's second home, and, as with any good regular, everybody knew her name.

It was one thing to spend time in bars; it was another to live there. At the age of seven, Tammy's mother disappeared from the streets of Martinez; nobody knew where she went—not the bartenders, not the town drunks, not the police. Desperate in the way that only lost children can be, Tammy ran from bar to bar, hotel to hotel, looking for the familiar figure of her mother, even wishing for the smell of alcohol and the yelling and cursing to give her a sense of belonging. The feeling of abandonment spread throughout her young heart until she cried out in pain and confusion. After weeks of searching, feeling more and more desperate, abandoned and alone, Tammy gave up looking and began fending for herself. At the age of seven, she began her life on the streets.

Martinez was a small Bay Area town whose sole reason for being was a nearby oil refinery that belched black smoke into the California air. The refinery wasn't just a workplace, it was a club. Many of the men who worked there were single, semitransient, and sometimes ex-criminals. During their shift, they could be found at the refinery doing their duty, making a quiet buck to take home to their small houses or hotel rooms. But when the shift was over they populated the bars, where they drank off the tensions of the working day and let their minds roam over whatever pleasures they could find in the small town.

By this time, because of her mother's addiction and the company she kept, Tammy was already addicted to heroin. With her mother always in a drunken rage or stupor, Tammy had been living one step ahead of total abandonment for years, and the drugs had helped soothe the situation. She was in and out of school, mostly without supervision from any responsible adult and always without love and affection from anyone. Now that she was utterly alone, the drugs were her only resort, the only thing she could count on, and her addiction—which even she did not understand—got worse.

The devil had wrought havoc in the life of one of God's precious creatures. It hadn't even been a fair fight—the Prince of Darkness versus a seven-year-old girl. Heaven, at the time, seemed inattentive. But though His heart was breaking, God had His eye on Tammy, and He was not letting her go, not until she had another chance in another place, a town called Modesto. It was a place that didn't even occur to a young mind clouded with heroin, but a place where God intended, after years of preparation, to deal a blow to the devil's head and recapture His lost lamb, who was crying in the streets of Martinez.

Chapter 4

"Boom-Boom" Meets the Quarterback

My freshman year at Louisiana Tech I moved into the all-football dormitories, and my new friends quickly caught onto the fact that I was a radical. I gladly accepted that characterization. I did not want to be known as a phony. To me, life was not milk and water, it was high octane gasoline, and I was determined to go as fast as I could.

Our football team made that possible for me because we were among the best in the country. Before I graduated we would win two national championships. I remember every one of the guys I played with—their strengths and weaknesses, their looks, their personalities—and we bonded together as a team, as a fighting unit, as brothers in arms. We worked hard for our success, practicing many hours a day, living, breathing, eating, and sleeping football, and because we were the football team, we stood apart from the other students. We ran together on the field and off. We were all-around zealots out for fun, living hard, going after the fast times and the parties just as much as we went after the big score in the big game. All of us, that is, except for Denny Duron, our quarterback.

Denny was different. He was a Bible-believing, straight-talking Pentecostal preacher's son from Shreveport, Louisiana. He had been preaching around the country since he was sixteen years old and was on fire with the gospel. I remember the first time we met.

"Are you Boom-Boom?"

"Yeah," I said.

"I have heard a lot about you."

"That's great."

"Are you saved?" he said, looking me right in the eye.

Saved? I thought. *What was that supposed to mean?* For the first time in a long time, I was caught off guard.

"Saved from what?"

"Are you born again?"

Still I had no idea what he was talking about.

"I'm Catholic," I answered.

"Well, are you a Christian?" he asked. "Have you confessed with your mouth and believed with your heart the Lord Jesus to be saved? You know, all have sinned and fall short of the glory of God."

"I'm not a sinner," I said. Then I went on the offensive. "I heard you were a preacher's kid, Denny. Don't worry about me. Things are different where I grew up in southern Louisiana. We were raised differently, that's all."

Then I got away from there quickly. What a strange introduction! Who was this guy anyway?

It got stranger when Denny started a Bible study in his dorm room. Two other players attended—for a grand total of three. I, on the other hand, had become a starting player as a freshman, so now I was hanging around with the big boys. At every team meeting Denny would announce his Wednesday night Bible study and invite everyone to come, and then I would stand up and announce the party that Friday night, and everyone would cheer and shout and get all excited. In no time flat I became Denny's biggest nemesis.

But he kept after me: "Boom-Boom, have you thought about what I told you? That you have got to confess with your mouth and—"

"Denny, I don't want to hear all that!" I'd say. "I'm a good person, I ain't no sinner, so quit telling me I'm a bad person."

"Well, do you believe that everyone who is a good person is going to heaven?" he asked.

"Sure I do," I said. "And I believe in God. Do you get that? I believe in God."

"The devil believes in God and he is not going to heaven," he said.

I didn't have a good response for that, but we continued to go at it, back and forth. I went out of my way to irritate him with my worldly, cool-guy attitude, and he tried to preach the gospel to me all the time. I could not get away from him because we were on the same team and had to practice together every day. It was maddening! To make it worse, his dorm room was situated so that you could not help seeing it when you came down the hallway.

It was not long before Denny posted his "Top Ten Most Unsaveable People at School" list on his door, and "Boom-Boom Berteau" was number one. That annoyed me a little bit, and I tore it down, but he had prepared for that by mimeographing the list—the next day it was up again. I didn't like it, but there was not much I could do about it. The other guys and I made fun of his little Bible group and warned freshmen away from Denny.

"Watch out for Denny. He's weird," we would say. "He does not believe in having any fun, poor guy."

But, of course, the reason I was resisting Denny's efforts was because they were new to me, and they challenged my ideas of what religion was. All the things he spoke about, even the idea of salvation, were utterly foreign to me. I thought religious talk like that belonged in dusty old theological books stuffed way back in my grandmother's attic, not in a college dorm room, and certainly not on the football field.

I had grown up in a Catholic family down in the southern part of Louisiana. My whole family was close. We knew our first, second, and third cousins, all our uncles and aunts, in-laws, grandparents, and everyone else. We were all Catholics. I was christened as a baby, was confirmed as a young man, learned all the prayers, and did all the other stuff that comprised "being a Catholic." My folks even sent me to a Catholic school, until I failed religion class.

The "spirituality" I had as a young man did not mean much to me; in fact, it meant nothing. It was dead, boring, a humdrum affair that I regarded like an insurance policy: I took care of it once and I didn't have to worry anymore because it was secure.

At the age of fifteen I stopped going to church. I was happy to forget my Catholic roots and strike out on my own to be the man I wanted to be, without Mass and all of that business encroaching on my schedule. The last thing I wanted to hear about was sin or conviction or even redemption, because I thought it was a sure thing: I was going to heaven. Why bring it up anymore?

So here I was gearing up for the college experience, the most exciting (I thought) years of my life—with athletic fame, freedom to live how I wanted, and freedom to make my own decisions—and Denny Duron wanted to talk about the status of my eternal soul! What did that have to do with anything, and who was he to be so impolite as to mention it in public?

At the end of the first year, Denny came down to my room.

"I may not see you next year," he said.

"Why?" I said, "Can't take it? You a quitter, Denny?"

"No," he said, and adopted a somber look. "The Rapture."

He looked up at the ceiling so I thought he'd said "rafters." I made the mistake of asking what he meant. He got in his preacher's stance, pointing his finger and carrying on.

"The Rapture! Ohhhh, brother! That is when Jesus will appear in the clouds, and in the twinkling of an eye He's gonna cause all those who are saved to be caught up with Him and to live with Him forevermore! And those who don't go in the Rapture are going to burn in hell

23

forever," he said. Then he looked deep into my eyes. "You want to go with us on the day of the Rapture?"

"No, Denny," I said. "I'd love to go with you into the clouds, but I can't. I have got to finish school, and my mom'll get mad if I go into the clouds too quick."

Denny was not impressed with my unconcern, but his little Rapture lesson set him up for a lot of jabs: "Denny's going to go in the clouds. Tell us before you leave, Denny, so we can wave good-bye." But in reality he was so believable when he said such crazy things that when we came back for sophomore year, I went down to his dorm room to see if he was still there. When I saw him sitting at his desk I had a pretty good laugh.

"You still here, aren't ya? You know why you are here? You got left behind, Denny! You've got sin in your life too!" I crowed.

That was all it took for him to post his top ten list again, and this time he even marked my name with a yellow highlighter.

Denny kept his Bible study going again that year, with a crowd of three every week. Meanwhile, I was living it up as best as I could with everyone else, but for the next two years he kept working on me, and there was not much I could do about it.

Up until this point I had never seen anyone be transformed by the gospel. I had seen someone who was already transformed, Denny himself, but I'd never seen anyone go from old to new. Then a friend of mine, Johnny, began hanging around with Denny a little too much, so I came to his room one night to get him to go to a party with us. There was an open Bible on his desk.

"Johnny, what are you doing?" I asked.

"I'm reading the Bible."

"Didn't I tell you to stay away from Denny?"

It turned out that he had been saved, and he told me what had happened in his heart. I got mad and chewed him out pretty well because now Denny was taking my friends away. And when they got saved, they started bugging me about getting saved too, and I didn't want anything to do with it.

But that, really, was just the exterior of my life. I didn't admit it to anyone, but slowly their message was beginning to sink in. I asked myself, *Was I really saved? Was I going to heaven? If I wanted to go to heaven, who did I need to talk to? What kind of deal could we make?*

One night, two days before a group of us were going to a big beach party in Galveston, Texas, I had a dream. For me, it was a Saul/Paul experience: It was shocking and life-transforming. I don't have visions or dreams like some people do, but that night I had a dream that was real. I dreamed that we were driving to the beach party, drinking in the car, having a good time, when my friend lost control of the car. The car rolled over, hit a tree, caught on fire, and we died.

I stood before a big gate, and God was there blocking it. I was waiting for Him to move out of my way, but He wouldn't budge.

"Here I am. I made it," I said. "Guess I'll go in now."

"Who are you?" He asked.

"Who am I? It's Boom-Boom. You know me."

"I don't know who you are," He said sadly. "When I look at your heart I don't see Jesus."

I was stunned and hurt by His words, and I immediately reacted.

"You know, if You would have told me what I needed to do, I would have done it," I said. "I would have done exactly what You said, but You never told me."

"I did tell you," He said. "I sent a fellow named Denny Duron."

"Denny was speaking for You?" I asked.

"Did he not say, 'God's Word says'?" God asked. "I was speaking through him to you."

At that moment a trapdoor had come loose beneath my feet. I went from utter light to utter darkness, seeing nothing and feeling the heat getting warmer and warmer around my body as I descended. Then I woke up.

I was drenched with sweat, and I got up to put water on my face. For the first time in my life, at twenty years of age, I realized that I was not going to heaven. All of my little excuses, all of the games I

25

had played that I thought would get me there didn't matter. I had not done what God said to do. I tried to blow the experience off the next morning, but my heart was very tender. I was feeling insecure, vulnerable, guilty—and convicted.

I didn't know that Denny and Johnny were plotting against me in the next room. They were targeting people they wanted to see saved and praying for it to happen. Johnny, being a new Christian, had not learned to doubt yet.

"I want to pray for Boom-Boom to be saved," he said.

"All right, we'll pray for that," Denny said.

"No. I want to pray for Boom-Boom to be saved at tonight's Bible study," Johnny said.

"Well, then, why don't you pray?" Denny said. For three years I had refused to come to their Bible study, and by this time Denny had come to see me as a long-term project, not an instant salvation. Now Johnny made it his personal mission to get me to come to the Bible study and to get saved. As soon as they were done praying, Johnny came right down to my dorm room and said, "If you come tonight, I'll never bother you again."

On those conditions I agreed to go. They had convinced a lot of guys to come as well, but clearly I was their biggest catch. When I walked into the room, proud and defiant, everyone looked at me. I was there. Boom-Boom had come to the Bible study.

The word Denny preached that night pierced my heart, and I knew I was not going to heaven. I knew I had not made a commitment to Jesus, and Denny drove the point home with his pointed, passionate preaching. At the end of his service, a number of the other guys raised their hands to be saved, but I, defiant and bullheaded to the end, held out. The meeting ended, and everyone went back to their rooms, but it was not over for me—Denny and Johnny followed me back to my room. They knew I was being convicted, that I was in knots inside, tied up and angry, feeling the heat of the Holy Spirit and trying not to give in. As I saw them following me to my room, I turned around and exploded.

"I don't want to get saved! I demand that you leave me alone this instant! Go!"

I was scared to death that their preaching would finally get to me, that I would crack, break down, watch my whole tough-guy image come falling down piece by piece in front of all those I had wanted so much to impress. But then the dream came back to me in its full reality, the one that had shaken my soul, and I realized that no matter what else happened, I didn't want to go to hell. I softened and allowed them to talk to me, and they spoke confidently of abundant life in Jesus, a life better than I had ever known, and then told me I needed to accept Him. At that moment I was completely broken, I had reached a point of total decision. It felt like God slapped me down on my knees to finally acknowledge Him as my Lord and Savior.

After three years of fighting it, I allowed Denny to lead me in prayer in that dorm room, and I felt Jesus come into my life. For the first time I knew that what Denny had been talking about was real. It was real! When I repeated the part about Christ forgiving me of my sins, I felt twenty years' worth of bottled-up sin pour out of my body and soul, and I knew that I would never be the same.

From that day forward, I was a radically different person, not a phony but an on-fire Christian with a different agenda and different goals than I had had before. The Lord had struck me down, and now He was going to rebuild me in His image, no matter how painful, no matter how long it took. It was the beginning of a long road that I could never have envisioned, never even dreamed of, when I first set foot on that Louisiana Tech campus.

Chapter 5

A Season for Hatred

oug Adams loaded a fresh magazine into his pistol, placed it in the holster, and stepped out the door of his home, squinting at the sun. Dull green and black tattoos covered his arms—three were of the Grim Reaper, one was a paratrooper tattoo, and one was the flying skull emblem of the Hell's Angels. With only his white T-shirt on, his chest could be seen through the faded white fabric. A scar ran from sternum to navel—brutal, half an inch wide, the kind that had healed with knots of tissue lining the incision, a crude mockery of a pearl necklace.

He scratched his chest absentmindedly near the scar. *Another day in the life,* he thought. *Nothing more than another day . . .*

Doug was a Grand Wizard for the Ku Klux Klan. Normally he wore black from head to toe, including a broad-rimmed cowboy hat, dark sunglasses, black jeans, and a handlebar mustache. He was a walking miracle, in his own way. The fact that he was still alive defied all the odds, considering the countless altercations he'd been in, the war he'd lived through, and the life he'd led, which was shot through with violence. He'd crisscrossed the country, putting thousands of miles on his motorcycle, living the life of a biker bandit—a life he cherished the same way he cherished his guns, polishing them like fine diamonds. Before becoming a Klan member he had been a Green Beret in Vietnam, and before that, a sixteen-year-old boy with twenty-nine grand theft auto convictions.

For Doug Adams, living beyond the laws of society was the only life he knew.

He leaned against the house and looked across the rooftops that made up the Modesto skyline. Somewhere behind his house the schoolkids were at recess, playing on the big open field. Doug listened to their cheers and squeals, and his heart softened for a moment. He loved children. He loved them because they had what he always wanted but never got: a home, a family, innocence . . . After a moment he cut the contemplation and walked back into the house where fourteen jugs of ether-based liquid were waiting to be cooked into crank. Before starting, he took an eighth of a gram of the drug and shot it into his arm . . . waited for the effect to hit. . . then got to work.

Yep, he thought. *Just another day in the life.*

Doug's childhood began and ended on the day he was born. Given up to foster care as an infant, bouncing from one home to another (seven in all), he had seen the worst of humanity. Most of the homes were merely fronts for the parents to get money from the state to buy drugs and alcohol, and several of his so-called parents abused him in ways that he was not able to come to grips with until forty years later. There was no one to check on him in the homes, and his foster parents always sent back the monthly report: "Doug is doing well, send more money for clothes." But Doug never got the clothes; instead, his foster parents bought whiskey, and the little boy stood by and watched them drink it.

Doug began to carve out his own world within the one he'd been given. He started stealing food at the age of six and learned to take money from his foster parents' wallets and purses. As they beat and molested him, a knot of hatred in his soul began forming and tightening, but when he transferred to yet another foster home, a sudden solution to his problems presented itself. Two of his older foster brothers were riding motorcycles with the Hell's Angels, and they took him under their wing. Overnight, Doug went from powerless to powerful, unprotected to entirely secure. By the eighth grade he had become the mascot of the local outlaw biker club, who called him "little preacher" because he would stand up to anyone and tell it like it was. Doug Adams was afraid of no one. He began stealing motorcycles, even police vehicles, for the local chop shop. Harley Davidsons were easy to get rid of; he just broke them down to their component parts and sold them.

More important, his "brothers" taught him how to be aggressive and take control of situations, how to take control of life. He would walk into a bar and throw the first punch in order to start a fight with rival biker gangs. His chapter, Hayward [California] Hell's Angels, often fought the Gypsy Jokers from Oakland at the dividing line between the two cities. At the age of twelve he got his first Hell's Angels tattoo, the flying skull, an honor greater than he felt able to receive. He was young, he was skinny, and he had an attitude that could kill. Eventually, it would.

Running into trouble with the law was inevitable. At the age of fifteen a judge they called "the hanging judge" hauled Doug into court, presented him with a list of thirty different violations, and gave him the choice between doing thirty-five years in jail or going into the military. Doug chose the latter, and the decision changed his life, but not necessarily for the better. He became a member of the Army Special Forces—a Green Beret, a trained killer—and suddenly, with the Vietnam War upon them, he had an outlet for his hatred and violence. The army not only taught him how to kill, but encouraged him to do so.

Doug had very little of his conscience left by the time he arrived on the battlefield, but the incident that robbed him of his ability to feel any emotion came when he rescued a two-week old South Vietnamese baby from enemy territory, carrying her fifteen kilometers to safety. He put her in a Catholic school and adopted her as his own. For six years he showed love to the girl, the kind that he had never received as a youngster. But then, in a senseless attack on civilians, she was killed by the Vietcong in a territorial scuffle, and Doug was deprived of the only person he had ever offered his unconditional affection. The only thing that remained was a dirty black-and-white photograph of the little girl posing in front of an army supply truck. From that point on, he felt nothing, and took on the role of "devil in the baggy pants," as Special Forces had been called in World War II. As part of the demolition unit, he and his buddies had the authority to roam around blowing things up. With hatred in his soul, Doug spearheaded deadly campaigns into enemy territory, perpetrating the kind of meaningless horror that had wrecked his own life. Whenever he shot one of the enemy soldiers, he nailed a Green Beret patch to the dead man's forehead and put an ace of spades in the hole where the bullet had exited—a trademark of death signifying that his battalion had been there. When a member of his six-man team turned back out of fear, he shot him out of respect for a rule of war: Never turn chicken, or you're dead.

Doug did more than sixteen hundred jumps during six years in the war. Vietnam left him scarred, inside and out. He was held for two and a half years in a POW camp, where he experienced unspeakable torture. He saw his friends dismembered and forced to eat their own flesh. His mother and father were officially informed by the army that he was dead. (His name is on the Vietnam Memorial Wall in Washington, D.C.) When he was released from the POW camp he weighed eighty pounds and had to be carried on a stretcher. On his first tour of duty, before being taken captive, he was shot in the head during an ambush; the bullet entered the base of his head and came out near the forehead. But somehow he survived and has a metal plate that goes from his forehead to the back of what used to be his skull.

He went for three tours of duty, and he came back to civilian life obsessed with violence, without emotions, and full of a hatred that defined his very character. Two years of his life he had lost for no explainable reason; they simply disappeared from his memory. Then he began riding with the Hell's Angels again, taking his Harley from Seattle to New York, San Francisco to Miami, stopping in biker bars that dotted the highways and byways of America. If one of the locals gave him trouble, Doug put one of his many guns to the local's face: "I'm not here to play games. I'm here for a couple of days, then I'm out of your town. Leave me alone or I'll kill you." Sometimes he had to shoot one of them to show he meant business. He never second-guessed his violent actions; in Vietnam, thinking about something too long meant delay and death. There was only action and reaction—no thought, no conscience. It was the way he had been trained to live from the time he was twelve years old.

Riding with the Hell's Angels brought him into contact with Ku Klux Klan members, and they piqued his interest. He was already sympathetic to their cause because of an incident that happened state-side during a leave of absence.

They were in a bar in California when Doug recognized a fellow Green Beret, a black man with whom he had gone through the worst battles and whom he trusted like a brother. The bar, it turned out, was mostly black, which didn't bother Doug; he liked people of all colors, and his friend was there if anyone gave him trouble. But when a group of black men approached him as he sat at the bar drinking, Doug appealed to his friend for help, but the friend shook his head and stepped back from the situation. "You're on your own," he said and turned away, allowing the men to beat Doug and throw him out onto the street.

A cardinal rule of loyalty had been broken, and inside his heart Doug felt a new hatred developing: a hatred for black men and women, based on the betrayal of a black man for whom he would have laid down his life.

He joined the Klan in 1982 and became their Grand Nighthawk—the grand enforcer, the assassin responsible for instilling fear by way of violence against those who frustrated the Klan's work. He had eight thousand nighthawks, or junior assassins, underneath him, waiting for his order to retaliate against anyone who came up against the Klan. As the bodyguard for the top brass (including David Duke) he was never without a gun or a knife at his side or in his belt, and he was ready to use them both. If you messed with him, he would ask if you wanted to be shot, stabbed, or have your legs broken, and then he would do it. As Grand Nighthawk he was the only Klansman in the country to wear a specific type of red and black robe, and to add to the effect, his robe was hand sewn by witches. Violence was his line of work, and few disputed that he was the best.

As Doug sat in the garage of his Modesto home smoking a cigarette, he watched the liquid cooking into fine white powder. Stretching out and leaning back in a folding chair he mused about the upcoming cross-burning they would hold outside of Modesto. He couldn't wait to be there, strutting his stuff in the robe only he could wear, flashing his firearms, and saluting the cross as it burned bright against the night sky. Little did he suspect that soon—sooner than he could have imagined—his life of crime would catch up to him . . . with a vengeance.

Chapter **6**

Fear and Despair

fter Tammy's mother had left Martinez without a word of warning, seven-year-old Tammy had made her home wherever she could: on muddy creek beds, in alleys full of rotting trash, in public parks among the bushes, and under barstools. The only friends she had were her mother's old drinking partners, the unruly riffraff of Martinez. When her mother left, they took pity on her and cared for her in some ways, providing meals and shelter when it was needed.

But they also took advantage of the young girl, demanding sexual acts in return for their so-called kindness. For the next three years Tammy engaged in child prostitution to keep herself alive. The men would take her up to a nearby park where the bushes and trees would hide them, or to a second-rate motel room with cigarette-burned sheets and threadbare carpets, and perform acts unutterable in heaven or earth. With her child's logic Tammy reasoned that it was her obligation to engage in whatever perversities they forced on her. They were, after all, the adults, and adults were supposed to know how things worked. She barely understood what was happening, but she knew it was wrong—she knew it by the oppressive feeling of guilt that surrounded each encounter. She knew she was being abused, but she also knew that giving them what they wanted was her ticket to a meal and a warm bed to sleep in. Survival was her one shot at security, and for a little girl with no one to protect her, security was worth any price.

With her mother gone, Tammy's dependence on drugs increased. She used whenever she could, getting her fix from the men in the bars who took advantage of her. She stole food from the store, stole anything she could get her hands on. She got money wherever she could, and at the age of eight she beat up another boy on the streets so badly that the police hunted her down and put her on indefinite probation. But, for reasons she never learned, they didn't rescue her from her squalid situation. They didn't take her off the streets or out of the bars or away from the pedophiles. Even jail or juvenile hall would have been better than the streets. Apparently the police were there to punish her, not to save her.

At the age of ten, a mixed miracle took place. Tammy's mother reappeared out of nowhere. She said that she had been to Reno, that she had a house and was going to go straight, which meant no more drinking and no more abandonment. The child whom the streets had made old moved in with her mother again and tried to lead a normal life: going to school and believing the promises her mother made. She took comfort in the thought that it was all going to be different. For the first time Tammy tasted hope.

But the promises were not kept. Her mother began drinking heavily and spending all of her time in the bars, and then one night, she brought home a man, another one of her drinking buddies. But he stayed the night and began to make himself a frequent visitor in their home. He came over to sleep with Tammy's mother, to drink with her, and to have a few laughs. He was fifty-two years old, and he already had a wife and a family of his own.

It was not long before he first sexually abused Tammy. Then he did it again and again and again. He began to come over for the express purpose of taking the little girl into the bedroom and having his way with her, and though Tammy's mother knew it was going on, she allowed it to happen. The man dropped by whenever he cared to—on the way home, on his way to work, on the weekends—and Tammy never resisted him. In a perverted way, he became Tammy's father figure. He paid the rent on the house; he stocked the kitchen; he kept her mother home from the bars, buying her enough alcohol so she would never have to go out drinking. Tammy felt she had to repay him because he was their protector, giving them more security than they had ever known, while exacting a terrible price from both women.

When Tammy was thirteen she became pregnant with his baby, and her mother and the man forced her to get an abortion. It was as traumatic as anything she could bear—the clinic, the doctors in their masks with their metal instruments, the humiliation and shame, the procedure itself. Even at that young age she mourned the loss of her baby.

Tammy's ability to stick it through had been forged early on, like iron in a factory furnace. She made it through high school long enough to get her diploma, trying to put on the act of a normal life though she was under the influence of alcohol or heroin most of the time. The other kids made fun of her ragged clothes and shoes, but their taunts only made her more determined to show people she could at least accomplish something.

At the age of seventeen Tammy gave birth to her first child, a boy named Jack. He was the child of the same man who had abused her over the years. At the age of nineteen she gave birth to her second boy, Earl, by the same man.

But in 1984 Tammy finally reached her limit of abuse. She packed up her car and drove away, leaving behind the man who had controlled her for eleven years. She was twenty-two years old. She had two children, a fifteen-year-old drug habit, and arms lined with dark splotches—track marks. She drove and drove, with no real direction, heading eastward away from the ocean toward the Central Valley and, further beyond, the Sierra Nevada mountains. The highways that connected the Bay Area to the Napa Valley, the Sacramento Delta to the Central Valley, blurred together as she ran the phrase over and over in her mind: *This time it's going to be different. This time I'm not going back. This time it's going to be different. This time I'm never going back . . .*

Tammy ended up in Stockton, an agricultural city with a port connection to the San Joaquin River. Her mother had remarried a decent man over the years, settled down as best she could, and let life go on. The man she had married took pity on Tammy and helped her to rent a house and establish her home in Stockton. For the first time in her life Tammy felt like she had a shot. Maybe it wasn't a shot at greatness, but at least a shot at goodness, a shot at a decent life, maybe a decent relationship . . . and finally, some peace.

But the years ahead would prove a double-edged sword, cutting her free from the past, but cleaving her heart with pain that needed more than a change of circumstance to heal.

Chapter 7

Rebellion, American Style

J avier Macias and his friend Tom skipped the last three periods of school in order to come back to Javier's place.

"I just bought a bag of weed. Let's get out of this place and smoke it," Tom had told him in between classes, standing amidst the crush of students getting to their rooms on time. Javier didn't care if he arrived to class on time; he didn't care if he arrived at all. School was a social excursion at best and an annoyance at worst. He was always ready to ditch for any good reason, or any bad reason for that matter.

"All right, I'll meet you out front," said Javier. "Let me get my backpack."

The two thirteen-year-olds slapped five and parted ways for the moment. As Javier walked down the now-empty hallway, one of his teachers caught sight of him.

"Javier, class has started," she said. Javier ignored her.

"Javier, you are as close to failing as anybody I've taught. I'm telling you now, you're right on the line. If you start coming to class, at least I'll give you consideration for that."

"I'm not interested," Javier said, not even looking back as he pushed the door open and stepped outside into the open air. "Not interested at all," he muttered to himself.

At Javier's house, he and Tom found their dope pipes in a shoe box in Javier's closet.

"Time for a good ride," Tom said.

Javier took a pinch of marijuana out of the bag and looked at it for a moment. How strange that such a magical little plant could give him such pleasure, and how easy it was to get at school. He thought back to the first time he and a friend had gotten hold of marijuana joints and smoked them behind Javier's house. He had felt guilty, but there was also a secret feeling of exhilaration, release from family problems, release from the responsibility he had for his little sister, release from the schoolteachers who always hounded him.

If there was one thing Javier Macias wanted it was to get away to a better life, away from his quarreling aunt and uncle, his surrogate parents, and the crushing stress of coming home to constant bickering. If he had a good family, he thought, maybe things would be different. Maybe he wouldn't need the drugs, the sex, the gangs. If he had a real family, maybe answers would be easier to come by and he could have someone to confide in about all the thoughts racing through his adolescent brain. As it was, he looked to his friends for acceptance. The answers they offered came in little baggies of dope, alcohol bottles, and parties where the music blared and girls invited the boys into dark rooms.

Javier lit up his pipe and pulled the first drag of smoke into his young lungs. He felt the scorching feeling, then the calming effect, blanket his body. Tom was already giddy, laughing and rocking on the bed. "Cool, man. I love this. Cool . . . " he said, lost already in the drug haze. It took longer for Javier, considering he'd been smoking marijuana for two years already. He wasn't a daily user, but when it came around in the groups he ran with, he was the first to volunteer.

Leaning back against the wall of his bedroom, the shades closed, the door locked with a towel shoved against the crack, Javier let the drug's effects consume him. He had come a long way from being a little boy in Central America. His story sometimes read like a bad soap opera. For a boy still three years away from the legal driving age, there was a lot to tell.

He was born in Guatemala City, Guatemala, when his mother was just a young woman in love—a tragic figure whose mistakes would drag her further and further down until she finally disappeared from Javier's life altogether. Javier's father was no better; he fled the family soon after Javier was born, for reasons Javier did not know. Many times he wondered why his father had abandoned them. Did he hate his mother? Did he hate the baby he had produced? Did he fear responsibility and the domestic life? Or was he simply a playboy, skipping from one young, beautiful girl to the next, leaving broken homes in his path? Javier didn't know. Perhaps he would never know. His origins had been lost in time and in memories nobody cared to recall.

His mother remarried, and his stepfather, a seemingly more responsible man, decided to make a break from Guatemala and move the family to California, the United States—the promised land across the border where everybody had televisions and was rich and drove a nice car. They had seen the vision on TV and in the movie theaters; they knew it was real. In order to scrape up the money, the stepfather came to the U.S. alone, and living with his sister who had just immigrated, he sent money to his wife and children back in Guatemala, hoping to eventually move the entire family. It was not their ideal condition; being separated was harder than both had imagined. Even the letters and the money could not make up for togetherness.

Slowly, over the months of separation, Javier's remaining family fell apart. His mother, driven by loneliness and made weak by romance and intrigue, became pregnant by another man. She made herself sick, worrying about what she would do should her husband call for them. She worried that she might give him some hint by her words in the letters she mailed him each week, so she stopped writing so many letters. Javier was too young to understand the betrayal that had happened before him, too young to understand love, passion, commitment, and broken trust. He only knew that he wanted a daddy and that he would get his daddy back when he made enough money to bring them to the United States.

Javier's stepfather sent for the family to join him in San Jose, California, while his mother was still pregnant with another man's child. Devastated, the woman moved to get rid of the problem, to pretend it had never existed and to claim the promise of a new life in America: she had an abortion. Her lover continued to call, but she wouldn't see him. Too late, she had decided to stay away. Now the memory of the abortion was etched in her mind forever, like a curse carved into an ancient stone.

The three of them—five-year-old Javier, his mother, and his three-year-old sister—got on a dilapidated school bus that was packed to the windows with families escaping third-world poverty and began the first leg of their journey to the United States. The bus traveled north through Mexico on roads half-paved and rutted, sometimes overrun with animals or mule-drawn carts. Occasionally, armed "federales" stopped the bus and made the people stand up against the bus while they searched them, taking money from those who had any to give and instilling fear in the rest by flaunting their machetes and machine guns, claiming ultimate authority over the roadways. The people, terrified, submitted to whatever happened, just hoping to escape and continue their journey northward. When the men yelled, Javier and his sister huddled around his mother's legs. His mother cried silently, her body shaking with sobs.

After countless hours of bumping and jolting and interrogation and intimidation, the bus reached the U.S. border. Not the border itself, where cars passed through a high-tech, eight-lane checkpoint leading from Tijuana to San Diego, but an old dirt road a few miles before the border, where no border guards patrolled and no one was there to check passports, let alone wish them a happy stay. There they left the bus and hooked up with their contact, a "coyote" who would sneak them into the U.S. In him rested their future, for if he failed, they would be left alone in Mexico, a foreign country to them. There would be a mother and two small children left to try and try again until they made it across. And even then, how would they find their husband and father? Who would help them? Certainly not the coyote, a mercenary who cared nothing for the people he sneaked across the border.

It soon became clear how the coyote worked and how the family would effect their passage into the promised land: in the dark, frightening trunk of a car, like so many other Latin American immigrants entering America in a shroud of secrecy and shame. With the assistance of U.S. citizens on the other side, they would slip past the border agents, hoping and praying to God above that the agents wouldn't open the trunk or sense anything suspicious about the driver.

They made it across successfully and were reunited with their father. But what should have been the beginning of a dream became the beginning of a nightmare. Instead of bonding together as a family in a new and exciting place, Javier's family disintegrated. His mother and stepfather separated after he found out about her affair, and Javier and his sister were left without a reliable guardian to care for them. They went to live with their aunt Sonia, a legal immigrant, in Modesto, because their mother didn't feel capable of caring for them in a foreign country where she didn't even speak the language. Javier and his sister felt like rag dolls, thrown this way and that, treated as if they were indestructible. Though the bruises didn't show on the outside, they were there on the inside, but there was nothing they could do to show it. They were just a couple of quiet, wide-eyed children shipped off to a stranger's house in a town they had never heard of. Perhaps the only familiar thing was the name of the city itself: Modesto, in Spanish, means "modest."

At least there was peace at their aunt's house. There was none of the tension of a husband and wife being torn apart by unfaithfulness. As children, they could sense the atmosphere between them. In Modesto, all was foreign, but all was calm, and for the moment the children preferred peace to familiarity.

But while they were in Modesto, their mother returned, against the will of their aunt, who knew their mother was in no condition to care for children. She came unbidden and kidnapped the children in the middle of the night while they were sleeping.

"Your aunt does not want you anymore," she whispered in their ears as she took them from their beds, bundled them in the car, and brought them to San Jose, where she was living virtually on the streets, doing whatever she could to stay alive.

Things would get worse. The children were virtually uncared for, unknown to the school system and the county government, unknown to anybody in the new world they were in. They never knew for sure if their mother was prostituting herself to make money; it wouldn't have occurred to their young minds. But one night while wandering through traffic, their mother was hit by a drunk driver and dragged several blocks down a main thoroughfare. During her hospitalization, the authorities had no idea what to do with the children, so Javier and his sister were put into an orphanage. Their stepfather had become an alcoholic because of the stress and grief his wife had caused him, and even if he could have cared for the children, he did not want them anymore. He had moved on to another life, one that had no connections to Guatemala.

Their aunt Sonia was the only one who stepped in on their behalf, bringing the children back to Modesto and treating them as her own. Their mother was soon deemed mentally ill and deported to Guatemala.

Things settled down with the stability of school and normal family life. Javier and his sister adapted to their new situation and treated their aunt and uncle as their own parents, and, as best as they could, they led the lives of everyday American youth, going to school, making friends, and playing games with others around their neighborhood. It was not until Javier Macias reached adolescence that he had to face more difficult situations in his life, situations that grieved him even more than the separation from his natural parents. His aunt and

43

uncle's relationship had gotten gradually worse over the years. Both were heavy drinkers, and they began to fight more and more often, sometimes becoming violent. One night, when both were drunk and angry, his uncle slashed Sonia with a kitchen knife across the chest and shoulder, and she had to go to the hospital for reconstructive surgery to repair the wounds.

But the wounds in young Javier's heart wouldn't heal so quickly. Seeing his uncle lash out was like being betrayed by his own father—the father he never had. He had trusted his uncle, admired him, patterned his own character after his. Now that example was gone. His aunt and uncle got a divorce, and Javier was left staggering with confusion over what had happened, and, as many adolescents do, he began to look for solace outside of the home. After all, he had been hurt by those he thought he could trust. Why not try something new? Why not rely on his friends for support? Why not do what everyone else was doing? When he was in the seventh grade, Javier was offered marijuana by a friend of his, and seeing nothing wrong with trying, he started a habit that would last most of his early life.

Sitting in his bedroom with Tom, Javier enjoyed the slightly sickening and delirious feeling of a marijuana high. In the back of his mind he was hoping his aunt wouldn't come home early and catch them. But he was getting bored with marijuana. It didn't give him the good feelings it used to. He had been asking around at school for other drugs, just out of curiosity; now he thought more seriously about it. He was a man now, he thought. He'd been making decisions for himself for years—even taking care of his little sister when no one else wanted them. Remember the orphanage?

"Hey, Tom, I think I'll get something harder next time. Maybe something like crank; I hear that's a trip," said Javier, gazing through the smoke. He thought about who he might talk to in getting the new drugs. Maybe he'd run into someone at a party who had some to spare for a first-timer. But Tom, laid out on the bed giggling, was in no condition to respond, which left Javier alone with his thoughts. It wasn't the first time, and it would surely not be the last.

Chapter 8

The Fall of a Star

remont, California.

Frank Tanner never thought he'd end up in Fremont, California. Austin, Texas, maybe, or Houston, New York City, or Nashville, the hub of the country music scene—someplace where dreams came true, not where they evaporated in the heat of a California summer. Fremont wasn't a bad city, true enough. In terms of income and quality of living it was somewhere between Oakland—gang territory—and Palo Alto—a university town with its intellectual elites. Fremont wasn't special one way or another, a San Francisco bedroom community, at best. Nothing spectacular. A suburb with a name.

Nothing Frank wanted was in Fremont. As he changed plates on the lithograph machine in the strip mall where he worked, he thought ironically to himself that he must be the only guy he knew who had failed at two promising careers. He chuckled to himself as he worked the machinery. Here he was, doing a job any high school graduate could do with three weeks' training. Frank Tanner, star material, his family's best hope, the pride of his father, was the only guy he knew who had missed out on stardom twice.

Professional disappointments came to everyone some time or another, but for Frank Tanner, they came earlier than to most. During his senior year of high school in small-town Ohio it was apparent that his dream of playing professional baseball was coming true. He shone on the field, playing head and shoulders above his own teammates, and well above any players who came through to challenge them. His eye was quick, his arm like a rope, and he could hit any pitch to the fence. He was the kind of player coaches would watch and shake their heads at in amazement; he was more than the run-of-the-mill high schooler—Frank had what it took to make a life out of the sport.

Playing baseball was the one thing Frank had dreamed of since he was six years old. Like so many other American boys he had lived baseball, breathed it, eaten it, slept it. He pictured himself on a baseball card, his statistics on the back. He pictured other kids collecting his face and bragging about his rookie card. His family had supported him all the way, coming to his games, buying him the best equipment, coaching him in the backyard until day turned to dusk. His dad especially had driven him toward lofty athletic goals, pouring his free energy into his son. Great expectations followed Frank all the way through his childhood and adolescence. His family, his school, his town knew he was going to make them proud. They knew he wouldn't fail them. Frank was going to the top.

Before he had even graduated high school he traveled thousands of miles from his hometown to try out for two major league teams who had scouted him the season before. Along with seven hundred other young men, he went through three days of total physical and athletic testing, designed to separate the good from the outstanding in as quick a time as possible. Each participant had to run the seventy-yard dash in less than seven seconds. If they didn't meet the standard, they were instantly eliminated and told to pack their bags and head home. Frank saw hundreds of bubbles bursting around him as young men like himself unceremoniously walked off the field and drove back to wherever they had come from, heavy with the knowledge that they would have to tell their family and friends that their bid for the majors had failed. Frank was confident enough in himself to put him a step ahead of most other participants, but he also had a healthy fear of being cut and taking the long walk toward the locker room. He thought of the expectations his father, coaches, and classmates had piled on him. He was counting on himself to come through for his father and for the whole town.

Frank kept up the pace among the several hundred would-be players who were left. There were reflex drills where a coach tossed the ball in the air and named the position it was to be thrown to once it was caught. Many more men were eliminated during the grueling exercise, fumbling the ball, throwing it to the wrong position, throwing it in the dirt. The coaches would accept nothing but perfection and didn't have time for anyone else.

"Number six, you're gone," they shouted, and another dropped out, walking humbly toward the locker room.

Finally, each remaining player had to step up to bat, not just against an elderly coach or another young prospect, but against a professional pitcher. It was the last exercise to weed out the remaining players who could not perform at a high professional level. Frank came to the plate and connected against the pitcher. Not only did he survive the tryout camp, he excelled. By the time it was over, he had made the final cut and attracted the serious attention of two major league clubs. He went home elated, the local Ohio boy making good; he was on his way to being the athlete and star everyone expected him to be.

But during his senior year of high school, still glowing with the prospect of playing in the major leagues, Frank made a mistake. In trying to keep up with his athletic regimen, trying, in his own words, to be the "all-around jock," he joined the football team and injured his knee on the gridiron. He had never even wanted to play football. It was just an exercise to keep him competitive, and, he had to admit, a way to stay in the public eye during the baseball off-season. As he lay on his back in the grass waiting for the ambulance attendants to come, he wouldn't allow himself to think that he had lost his shot at playing professional baseball.

But by the time the leg had healed, Frank's dreams were long gone over the horizon, like wild horses never to be seen again. For an eighteen-year-old athlete facing adult expectations, it was the single biggest disappointment of his life. Worse yet, it was the single biggest disappointment of his father's life, and it showed in his eyes. Reluctantly, Frank became a regular guy, trying to act and be like everyone else he graduated with—not a role he relished. He took a normal job to make a living. He went into the printing business, full-color lithographs and shop work. It was a far cry from the smell of freshly cut grass, the white-striped infield, and the fans in the bleachers. There wasn't anybody cheering him on now, and the only satisfaction was the paycheck.

Frank Miller's lifelong high had suddenly hit a low.

For a while he tried to resurrect the dream of professional sports during his time off, playing softball and double-A level baseball, seeing if he could get back in the groove and find his brilliance. Maybe he would get a call from a scout or an agent . . . But he knew in the back of his mind that it would never return. The promise had dissolved; Frank had blown it.

To get as far away as he could from his disappointments, he moved to California, leaving the small Ohio town behind. Frank had gotten married soon after high school, but his obsession with sports had driven away his first wife after seven years, and he often wondered if he would ever be allowed to dream again.

Then Frank was on the verge of a new career, one that had nothing to do with sports. Frank and his brother had sung together in church when they were children because their grandfather was a Baptist minister, but Frank had left the church at the age of fifteen after deciding that there were too many hypocrites involved in organized religion. In 1980 he and his brother put together an act and formed a band called the Tanner Brothers. They began to write songs together. Frank sang and played guitar; their voices blended as only the voices of brothers could. They had songwriting talent too, and everyone knew it, for in a few short years they were hitting the road to open for some of the biggest country acts on the scene: George Strait, Dolly Parton, and Mickey Gilley to name only a few. They had satin jackets, tour hats, and albums for sale, and they had promises from record labels in Nashville that they would record an album and become the next big thing on the country music scene. Once again, Frank's star seemed to be rising.

During this time Frank got on with other aspects of life as well. He got married and had a little girl, and his attention began to turn to family life. However impossible it may sound, he had held onto a printing job while the band was getting bigger and bigger. Then, after seeing several projects fall through and experiencing more than his share of music industry letdown, he quit the group. He wanted to spend at least a few hours a week with his daughter, and he was tired of the taxing lifestyle of professional music, always traveling, practicing, setting up, tearing down, and meeting with people whose promises were as thin as the money they said they could deliver.

Unfortunately, after he quit the band, Frank's wife quit him. She had been enamored with Frank when he was a music star, but when he quit the band they grew apart, finally divorcing. Frank went back to full-time printing. Once again, his hopes of stardom had been dashed, and he still was not living the kind of life he wanted to live. There were many questions, but no answers; there was disappointment, but no hope. He was fighting for his place in the world with two failed careers and two divorces, and he didn't know where to turn for stability or fulfillment.

Frank knew that when people walked into the lithograph shop in Fremont, they couldn't tell by appearances that he had once been a major league prospect or a country musician on the edge of stardom.

They saw only an average guy; he knew that, and it haunted him. As he finished up a job on a nondescript, sunny Friday afternoon, Frank reined in his thoughts, because when he allowed them to wander they always came back disappointed. It was better to play the part of the print shop hand, no more, no less. In reaching for stars, he had discovered, you were liable to get burned.

Chapter 9

From Louisiana Tech to the Pulpit

ebbie and I had started dating when I was a senior and she was a sophomore at Louisiana Tech. She had been saved at the age of seventeen, and we had met on campus before I was a Christian. In fact, after we first met, she and her friends went back to their dorm room and prayed for me to be saved! After I accepted Jesus, I went to Chi Alpha Christian fellowship meetings, where Denny gave a sermon every week, and Debbie was there. Eventually, Denny reintroduced us and prodded us to go on a date together.

It was not only the right place and the right time, but the right match. Debbie and I prayed together that the Lord would show us the right way and tell us if we were not supposed to be together, because we didn't want to hurt one another. We had a series of confirmations in our spirit that this was the right relationship, and one night I asked her to marry me. But the following day I was so alarmed, confused, and bewildered at my own rash decision that I could not remember what day it was, and I went to all the wrong classes. Despite that harrowing experience, our decision stood, and after I graduated we got married.

We stayed in Ruston and bought a house, and I decided not to pursue professional football and instead followed in my father's footsteps and became a salesman. My natural enthusiasm and persuasive ability served me well. I hit all the goals, gathering all the bonuses. I thought my career was off to a pretty good start.

But my conversion to Christ had been lasting and Debbie and I wanted to serve the ministry. So in our off-hours we started a weekend Christian coffeehouse with music, speaking, pizza and coffee—all the things that would attract people from the community. I also went around to local youth groups and told my testimony, played my guitar, sang a few numbers, and spoke from my heart. I was a great one-nighter, but my material pretty much ran out after that, which was fine by me. I had a career track already. I didn't expect my forays into ministry to become a way of life by any stretch of the imagination.

At the same time Denny Duron was traveling all over the country evangelizing, and after I had been in sales for two years, Denny pulled a surprise move on me: He recommended me for a post as youth pastor in Pasadena, Texas, just outside of Houston.

"You did what?" was my response when he told me what he had done.

I had not ever considered becoming a pastor of any sort; indeed the whole idea of making a living in "the ministry" was foreign to me. I could understand donating time as we had been doing with the coffeehouse, but I could not understand how pastors made money doing what they did. I guess my assumption up until that point had been that nobody really made a living in church work, they were simply volunteers. But I knew that as a salesman I could make a financial contribution to the church, buying them nice speakers and making sure the building looked nice. I thought the only way I could help the church was by being in business, making lots of money and donating it. As far as youth pastors were concerned, that was not my line of work at all. I thought they lived in the back of the church and spent their time rearranging hymnbooks.

But after some convincing telephone calls with Denny and some honest prayer on our part, we felt like it was the right thing to do—I took the job. It was my first real commitment to the ministry, taking on the Lord's work full-time. Debbie and I were like wide-eyed infants and our minds were like sponges, soaking in everything that we saw and heard. Because we had not grown up in the ministry, we had literally everything to learn, but we also felt like we had a lot to give, and as we sought the Lord's will we began to feel Him working in our hearts. He was building a dream in us—a vision. And the foundation for that vision began at our church in Texas.

When I began filling my role as youth pastor, I threw my entire life into it, working eighty hours a week and taking on so many tasks and jobs that I am surprised now that I did not drop dead after that first month. I was in charge of neighborhood outreaches and renting out the fellowship hall. I typed up the church bulletins, took them to the printer, folded them myself, addressed them, separated them into ZIP codes, and mailed them. I was in charge of maintenance and janitorial duties, making sure the church was clean. I did most of the music, and, to top it off, I was the coach of the softball and basketball teams. I did all this while also serving as the full-time youth pastor.

Young and zealous men often shoulder such a burden in the church, but I honestly thought I was doing the right thing. I thought it was God's will that I spend as much time as possible doing "ministry" things. And since I have always been highly motivated and success oriented, it did not seem unusual for me to put every waking moment into my work, just like I had done with football and sales.

Debbie saw it differently. She had grown up in a churchgoing home, but not a ministry home. There is a big difference. If a family is in the ministry, they are almost required to be at church every time the doors are open; they live in the spotlight, and their lives must be exemplary. When I first got into ministry, it was a real shock for Debbie, and the fast-paced, always-on-call life of a minister and his wife left a bad taste in her mouth.

Every hour I spent at work was an hour I could not spend with her at home, and the more focus I gave to the ministry, the more resentful she became of it. I was neglecting my wife, and I thought I was pleasing God. Ultimately, God led me to the Book of Haggai: "'You have sown much, but bring in little . . . You looked for much, but indeed it came to little; and when you brought it home, I blew it away'" (1:6,9). God was saying to me, *It's not how many hours you put in at the office, but what you produce with those hours.*

I had to look at my production. Was I able to show anything for all the extra hours I was putting in? Was I sowing much, but bringing in little? Was I judging my ministry with a time sheet instead of a production table?

The answer was yes. I was keeping myself busy, but that was not the measure of ministry. I realized that God says that if you don't take care of your own bride, you will not be equipped to take care of His bride, which is the Church. That was a major lesson I learned in Texas and would continue to learn over the next few years. I needed to balance the multiple responsibilities of job and family that God had given me, and when the ministry cut into my home life, I was to ask myself where my priorities were.

Chapter 10

Joining Jimmy Swaggart Ministries

*D*ebbie and I were youth pastoring in Orlando, Florida, in 1983 when we first got the news that Jimmy Swaggart Ministries needed a new youth pastor for their Family Life Center. By this time I was ready to get back to Baton Rouge, my old home country, to be near my friends and family, to be with people who spoke my language and understood the difference between crawfish and shrimp, gumbo and jambalaya. Swaggart's church was actually smaller than the one we were at, but he was putting a lot of energy into starting a Bible college to train youth pastors from around the country, and that fit perfectly with the desires of my heart. I had always wanted to train ministers but had not been in a situation where that was possible. Now, by joining a growing, worldwide ministry, I was putting myself in a position to influence youth ministry around the country—all from our central hub in Baton Rouge.

By the mid-1980s Swaggart Ministries was expanding by leaps and bounds. Swaggart himself was one of the undisputed kings of evangelism, due in large part to his television and tape ministries. People seemed to love everything he did, from taking on the major television networks on issues of morality, to preaching, to playing the piano. He had a great following. And there was a lot of vision in his ministry at the time, lots of room for people like me to follow our grandest dreams. There seemed to be no limits to what we could dream about, and Swaggart was always behind us. He peopled his staff with men who were driven, who saw a destiny in the work they were doing.

Before I accepted the position with Swaggart, I prayed about the decision and felt very strongly that I had received a word from the Lord in regard to my life and ministry. I felt Him telling me that I was to take the lessons I had learned in Texas and Florida and apply them in Baton Rouge so that He could prove to me and everyone else that biblical principles were immutable and would work anywhere and anytime if applied with faithfulness and diligence. I felt Him saying that in Baton Rouge the desires of my heart would finally be fulfilled after all those years of training and maturing, which, frankly, we had needed to bring us to the point where we could manage a large ministry. My time at Swaggart Ministries was going to be the pinnacle of my ministry. It was with Swaggart that Debbie and I expected to see our dream fulfilled, our dream of a city won for the Lord, of a great ministry to youth, of a platform from which to proclaim the Word of God. With all of the things that lay ahead of us in Baton Rouge, Debbie and I knew we were getting in on the ground floor of an exploding, exciting ministry.

When we first arrived in Baton Rouge and I assumed leadership of the youth, the meetings were running only forty to fifty youth each week. I saw great potential in those youth and in the resources we had, and through hard work and extensive outreach, in one year's time we had brought that number up to 550 youth every week. The more people came, the more exciting the meetings were and the more curious other youth were to see what was going on. Success bred more success, and we continued to push to take the city back from the devil. We put up posters all around the city, made T-shirts, and had a very effective word-of-mouth network at our schools; within just a few months there was not a young person in Baton Rouge who had not heard of CrossFire, the name of our youth group. We had campus clubs at all the schools, live bands at our weekly meetings, and a strong habit of worship and praise. I preached every week, targeting subjects that made a difference in their lives—peer pressure, sex, alcohol, teen relationships, and so on—and by getting down to their level, the sermons became that much more powerful. I can't remember a time when the altars were not full.

By our third year there, we had 1,400 youth coming to our meeting each week, and we were reaching every high school and junior high in the city. At the local college we had "Tiger Church" meetings (borrowing from their mascot), which attracted large numbers of college students who may have otherwise been sidetracked into life-destroying choices and philosophies. We were doing things on a scale bigger than I had ever seen. I wanted to make it worth people's while to come to a meeting, so things were dynamic and energetic rather than small and stagnant. We could draw more people that way and change more lives.

Not only that, but, as I had anticipated, God used me to train ministers from around the country. We began to organize regular youth conferences for youth leaders. Within a few years we had three thousand attendees, people from every state in the nation, coming to learn how to be effective in youth outreach. We were leading the nation with new and innovative ideas and were able to combine our teaching with real-life demonstrations of how to reach youth, using our own youth group as the model. We had classes to teach people how to lead worship at their meetings and fellowship groups, how to get on high school and college campuses, how to turn teenagers into soul winners. I put out leadership manuals and tapes and wrote a weekly column in the *Evangelist* magazine.

57

As part of my ongoing training work, I taught the youth ministry major at our Bible college every semester, and the men and women who went through those classes regularly went back to their churches and saw their youth groups double and triple in size. To me, that was the most important thing we had going in terms of youth ministry, sowing the seeds of successful youth ministry all over the country.

For four years the Lord built up our vision before our very eyes, and we rode the crest of a wave that seemed to be always gaining momentum. All of the things I had wanted to do—reach a city, train leaders, have a ministry that people could see—seemed to be coming to pass, and I was more than pleased—I was ecstatic. When you are living in the promises of God, you know that there is no other way to go; when you are receiving His bounty, it brings a feeling and satisfaction unparalleled by any worldly pleasure. We were sitting on top of one of the world's most impressive ministries.

And then, in the space of a tabloid newspaper headline, the tower was toppled and the dream came crashing down.

Chapter **11**

The Collapse of a Vision

On a Sunday morning in 1988, Jimmy Swaggart went on television at his usual broadcast and confessed to having sinned against God. The whole world watched their television sets; Debbie and I watched from our hotel room in Michigan where we were ministering. We had not expected any such thing to happen, and as we watched, we sat there, saying nothing, tears rolling down our faces. It felt as if we had gone out from Baton Rouge to extend the ministry we believed in and all of a sudden the extension cord was pulled from the main power center.

In my own mind I have often thought of that moment as the Hiroshima of evangelism, and we were at ground zero. Christians all over the world certainly felt the effects of it, but only in a distant manner, through reading the newspaper or watching television. But it is entirely different to read about a bomb dropping and to be there when it happens, as we were. The people who saw the bomb hit in Hiroshima have a whole different perspective than those of us who simply read about it in history books. As someone who was there when the bomb hit Swaggart Ministries, I simply cannot describe the devastation that we felt upon returning to Baton Rouge and sorting through what had happened. Before it ended it would shake the foundation of everything we had believed and lived for since we had first devoted our lives to ministry.

It quickly became a media frenzy, with mainstream and tabloid news outlets preying on the weakness of one Christian leader, and painting all Christians with that same brush. There was shame and hurt everywhere in the Christian world. I had *Newsweek* banging down my door, all the major newspapers, all the networks, Ted Koppell, Geraldo Rivera, *Hard Copy, Inside Edition,* and all the other trash TV shows were trying to get me to talk, to say something provocative or damaging. Even five years later they would come barging into our church with cameras rolling hoping to get some inside dirt and a spontaneous interview. I never gave it to them.

From that moment forward, our ministry was effectively over. Swaggart's multimillion-dollar operation did not just come unglued, it was like a straw house in a hurricane. There was total confusion: The shepherd had sinned and the sheep were scattering. In our personal lives, Debbie and I were beyond devastated. We felt abandoned and betrayed, like a child watching his parents split up; our trust was broken, our faith was questioned, our hearts were rent in the aftermath of human error. We had been running the largest youth ministry in the country, and we had done nothing wrong, but now everything we had worked for was gone. Our platform to the youth of Baton Rouge—gone. Our successful training seminars to youth pastors—gone. Our youth conventions—gone. As the wheels came off Swaggart Ministries, those of us who were going through it experienced personal destruction the likes of which I could not have imagined. My family experienced persecution and torment from those outside and inside the church. We were blasted from all sides, and amidst the ruins, the devil sent his powers of evil to sow even more destruction. I felt utterly victimized, spiritually raped.

Even so, we made the decision not to perpetuate the devastation that began with Jimmy Swaggart's admission of sin. We knew that God had not failed us—man had. Debbie and I sat down and mapped out our response very carefully, holding ourselves to God's standard of forgiveness, and we settled on some key principles.

- We wouldn't bad-mouth anyone else in the ministry.
- We wouldn't try to keep up with what was happening across town.
- We wouldn't allow any unforgiveness or bitterness to take root in our lives.
- We would pray for Jimmy Swaggart and his family.
- We would keep our eyes on what God had told us to do, and focus on our work in the church.
- We wouldn't take every occasion to defend ourselves against every attack.
- We wouldn't talk to the media. Ever.

Jesus' story about the unforgiving servant in Matthew 18 guided our attitudes and actions at that crucial time. The king in the parable forgave a servant who begged for forgiveness of millions of dollars in debt. Then that same servant went out and demanded repayment from a fellow servant and wouldn't forgive him, even though the debt was only a few dollars. At the end of that parable, the king "'was angry, and delivered him to the torturers until he should pay back all that we due to him'" (v. 34). Jesus continued, "So My heavenly Father also will do to you if each of you, from his heart, does not forgive his brother his trespasses" (v. 35). I, for one, did not want to be thrown to the torturers! Nor did I want to crack the foundation of my own ministry by allowing unforgiveness to stunt my spiritual growth, because whatever you do in times of crisis to other people will rebound on you. If you are faithful in those times, you will build a reputation for that, but if you bad-mouth people and try to scramble to salvage what you can for yourself, you will be known for what you are: a self-ish, low-down opportunist who does not care for the working of God's grace in that situation.

Thus began a period of five years—it felt like fifty—that Debbie and I have come to know as our own personally tailored trial by fire. The vision I had built up in my heart, the dream I had followed and which the Lord seemed to be fulfilling, was gone. Everything I had worked for was cleared off the table with one gigantic sweep of the hand.

We had to decide what to do with our future. Even though we left Swaggart Ministries we didn't leave Baton Rouge; we concluded that Jesus was needed most where people were hurting, and at that time, that place was Baton Rouge. There was a spirit of betrayal and distrust among churchgoers there, and a cloud of cynicism hung over the city. The peoples' attitude toward ministers was almost like, "Well, what is in your closet that we ought to know about?"

In this time of confusion, as my vision lay in pieces at my feet, I asked the Lord, "What good can come from this? Where do I go from here? Where do you go when you are brought back to square one and everything is in a pile of rubble?" In answer to that prayer of mine the Lord said, *Glen, man does not give you a platform. I give you a platform, so be faithful to me. Keep the dream alive, and I will give you a platform.*

Debbie and I believed that promise, guiding our lives by it, even while the pain lingered deeply in our hearts. My football training came back to me, because in football you never let anything beat you; you never give in. Playing sports breeds mental toughness and a mindset that says whatever happens, you are still in the game. At that time we decided that we would never quit. We decided that the only cure for a broken dream was to dream again, and that is how we were able to move past that life-shattering situation.

It is true that by coming through hard times the Lord makes us stronger, and my wife, Debbie, is a good example. God took the Swaggart experience and all the crushing experiences that followed and used them to create a burning desire in her for evangelism. She was truly transformed. She was no longer "resigned" to the ministry by any means. She was on fire with the Word of the Lord, developed a zealous desire to win the lost, and, like me, wanted to rub it in the devil's face as often as she could. But it took those years of attack to galvanize her spirit.

My heart, too, became stronger towards evangelism, but during that whole time I worried that our platform was being destroyed over and over again. What, after all, was I known for?

The devil tried to tell me that after having had a platform once, I could never claim the promises of God again. He told me that I got only one shot to make it work, that God had given up on me and I needed to give up on myself. Sometimes these lies were difficult to withstand, but still, I was not able to rest on my past. When things failed, I could not just say, "Well, I guess that was it. I will just live out my remaining years in some retirement home for over-the-hill preachers . . . " I have never been content with what I have done before. And I felt the Lord speaking to me again, clearing away the devil's lies: *Forget about what you did in the past that you thought was so cool,* He said. *I'll give you something far better. Put all that behind you and look ahead, because I own the past, and, more importantly, I own the future.*

I remembered the Lord's promise to give us a platform, I believed it, and I cultivated it in my heart. Even then I didn't know that He was just about to raise us up out of that time and restore the vision that had lain dormant in our hearts. He was already working in ways that we did not even know about, preparing a new place for us where we would find amazing victory in His promises.

Chapter 12

Down at Cagney's Bar

oug Adams drained his whiskey and deliberately set his glass on the bar, ignoring the man a few stools down. Usually no one in Cagney's bar bothered him; they knew what he was made of. But this guy was new and acting a bit stupid for being a stranger. He had made a few comments aimed in Doug's direction, comments that normally signaled an invitation to hostility. But though violence was second nature to him, Doug was careful when and where he would let it out of the box. He knew that once he'd made his decision, instinct would take over.

The bar's owner, Lane Cagney, eyed the new customer warily and washed out a used beer glass.

"I said I don't think you're as bad as you think you are," the man said again, looking at Doug.

"Don't get me mad," Doug said calmly, stroking the beads of sweat off his glass of whiskey.

"What?" the man said, tensing.

"I said don't get me mad. I guarantee you won't like me if I get mad," Doug said.

"What, is that some sort of threat?" the man asked, standing up from the bar and finally getting the kind of response he had been looking for. Doug shook his head and felt the familiar anger rising up within him. He stood up and faced the man.

"Now you've got me mad."

"Well, then do something about it," the man said, scoffing.

"Not in the bar. Outside," Doug said. He and the man walked toward the door, followed by a trail of patrons, including Cagney. They took a right, then another right, back where no one could see them, particularly the police. Squaring off in the dark, Doug sized up the man. He was big, but he wasn't fit. Doug, on the other hand, was wiry, thin. Not much of a threat by outside appearances, but what didn't show was that he was a killer by trade and could take a man's life as quickly as he could down a shot of whiskey. It wasn't hard if you knew what you were doing, and Doug did. In terms of military skill, he was a dream; in terms of civil society, he was a nightmare.

The rock hard blow hit the man's throat before he had even balanced himself, sending him to the dirt. Without pausing, Doug kicked him in the chest with his steel-tipped boots, then ground his bootheel in his face—his own personal signature. He didn't wear steel spurs for nothing.

The crowd behind him stood wide-eyed. They were used to prolonged, messy, unprofessional brawls, where the combatants groped and swatted at one another before catching their breath and walking back into the bar. Doug's performance had been so mechanical, without remorse, that they didn't know what to make of it. As Doug divided the crowd and walked back to his seat at the bar, Lane Cagney shook his head with a mixture of awe and horror.

"You don't have a conscience," he said.

"That's right," said Doug. "Nothing there. Nothing at all."

Lane shook his head again, brought another drink, and called an ambulance for the man out back, who still lay in the dirt bleeding.

Doug was a truck driver now. No more, no less. He had used to be a cooker; he made crank in a methamphetamine laboratory, right next to an elementary school. He shot up twice a day, a habit worth four hundred dollars. Then, in 1985, federal forces, who had been after him for ten years, closed off the block and laid siege to the house. Doug, with nowhere to hide, surrendered and was taken to prison, making the front page of the newspapers in the process.

He might have avoided the whole situation, but he had put himself in the public eye when he went to a cross-burning near Modesto, and the local newspaper showed up and took pictures of him standing in front of the burning cross with a fully automatic rifle. That had put the local police onto his trail and led to the federal bust.

He had spent five years in San Quentin, where he went cold turkey from drugs, had the snakes, the shakes, the sweats, tried to hang himself with his underwear, and slit his wrists before being released on parole. The only good that came out of his prison tour was a kicked drug habit. As for the knot of hatred, it had outgrown his heart and circled itself around his entire body, like a noose waiting to strangle him for good.

He became a drinker and a trucker, coming in drunk at seven in the morning and hauling equipment back and forth on Highway 99. He also became a regular at Cagney's bar, south of Modesto, where, because of his prowess, he came to be known as the bar's unofficial bouncer, breaking up fights, beating up troublemakers, and hurting anyone who got out of line.

One time a group of men had come by with their guns, ready to beat up one of the Cagney's regulars. Doug handed Lane his .38 Magnum, walked out to his truck, grabbed his .357, a 44 Magnum, and a couple of 25 automatics, and came through the front door of the bar.

"I'm ready to rock and roll," he said loud enough so the gang could hear him. Then he handed his extra guns to some of the regulars. "I'm going to kill these guys, watch out," he said, and he meant it, though the gang members were smart enough to leave before it could happen.

Not long afterwards a crazed man had tried to rob the bar at closing time and shoved a pistol in Doug's face. As Lane ran to call the police, Doug taunted the robber.

"You'd better pull the trigger now, because one of us is going to die," he said. "Come on! Pull the trigger! I'm just going to take it away from you and blow you away."

Part of Doug's heart was hoping he would fire the shot and end it for him. Doug called the gunman every name he could think of, but the man had frozen; he didn't know what to do. When fifteen cops showed up, Doug still wouldn't back down; he was angry that someone would pull a gun on him and not have the guts to shoot. And he was ready to prey on the weakness, just as he had in the jungles of Vietnam.

The cops finally subdued the man, and one of them pulled Doug aside.

"You are about the stupidest man I have ever seen," the cop said. "You stand up to a man who is stoned out of his mind and has a pistol pointed at your head."

"I don't care," said Doug, the scene still fresh in his mind. "I don't care how big he is, what weapons he has, or what he's on. I was in Special Forces for ten years. If he had come one step closer I would have taken the gun and killed him."

Though he was out of the Klan, out of prison, and out of the war, he was still in Doug Adams's skin. The only thing he had to his credit was the gang down at Cagney's bar, which was his home away from home. If ever he had felt affection for anyone, it was his drinking buddies, especially Lane Cagney, who bore an astonishing resemblance to Doug's own biological father. It was the one place where he could let his guard down and put the lid on the cauldron of hatred in his soul. At Cagney's, Doug could speak freely, laugh even.

He rocked slightly on the barstool as Lane served him another drink—complimentary this time, for taking care of a troublemaker. Doug was there to protect and defend his friends, just like he always had. What was loyalty, after all, if you didn't demonstrate it?

Chapter **13**

From Swaggart Ministries to Rodeway Inn

itting rock bottom puts you in the position of having to make something of nothing, which is a valuable experience for Christians. It forces you to see that you can't do anything on your own, that whatever you build of your own power will come crashing down sooner or later unless the very foundation was God's to begin with.

The first platform the Lord gave to us after the Swaggart debacle was in a Rodeway Inn outside of Baton Rouge where Debbie and I rented some lounge space, a few chairs, a public address system, and began a church. It was not glamorous, but I was not looking for glamour; I was looking to be obedient. I told God, "I don't care if my name is ever known by anyone else or is attached to any kind of earthly success. I just want You to be pleased with me." Our church met in one of the rooms near the lobby, a bar sort of area, and the only compliment I received while pastoring there was when a young boy came up to me and said, "Pastor, I just love your church. It's the only one in town with a pool. I told all my friends about it."

Even though it was difficult pioneering a church and starting from scratch, we did have some reasons for encouragement. We grew to four hundred people in six months and merged with another church to become Hosanna First Assembly. In the first year of our existence we were the fastest-growing church in the country. At the end of 1989, things seemed to be going along wonderfully. We were pastoring in a church with real buildings and facilities that we owned—no more hotel lounges or high school band rooms. We were growing by tens and twenties, and I began to feel the vision coming back in my heart. Perhaps we had been through the worst, and this was a time of rebuilding; perhaps we could dare to hope again that God would restore the vision of an evangelistic church winning a city for Christ.

I turned again to the Book of Habakkuk and read two of the verses that had become thematic in my ministry, and which I looked to as the great promises of God. The first one said, "'Look among the nations and watch—Be utterly astounded! For I will work a work in your days Which you would not believe, though it were told you'" (1:5). The second was in 2:2–3: "The Lord replied: 'Write the vision And make it plain on tablets, That he may run who reads it. For the vision is yet for an appointed time; But at the end it will speak, and it will not lie. Though it tarries, wait for it; Because it will surely come, It will not tarry.'"

I believed that one day we would watch and be utterly astounded at what the Lord was doing, and I believed that His vision would come at the appointed time. With all these things in mind I decided to do something I had never done before. I took literally the Lord's command to "write the vision and make it plain on tablets." At the beginning of 1990, and every year after that, I fasted and prayed about the vision God would lay on my heart for that year, and then I made up an overhead (only because stone tablets took too long) and listed all of the goals that made up the church's vision. On a Sunday in January,

I presented that to the church, and we guided our actions that year toward fulfilling that vision.

I explained that the future belongs to those leaders and churches with vision, because visionaries will always define the future. But a vision is not much if it is just a lot of grand talk—it must have specific components. It must not be held in secret by a leader; it must be presented to all the people of the church. The vision overheads I put up always contained very specific things: "We want a weekly ministry to twenty shut-ins; we want a budget of such-and-such size; we want a youth group of five hundred youth," and so on. "Make it plain," the verse said, so I made it as plain as I could. It was not just a lot of hot air from the pulpit; they were real, actionable goals that the church could work on as a body. "That a herald may run with it," the verse says, and before you can run, you must have somewhere to run to. As the pastor of the church, I saw it as my responsibility to provide the specific destination.

Not only did I fast and pray about that year's vision, but for a long-term vision, too, a ten-year vision. That vision was more important to me because it included all of the in-between years, and as I fasted and prayed, I began to write down what the Lord was speaking to my heart: We would have a twenty-five-hundred-seat sanctuary, twenty-five acres of land, a one-thousand-student Bible institute to train people for service in the ministry, a prayer chapel, a children's and youth sanctuary. Those were grand promises, but I believed they would come to pass, and I held them in my heart, anticipating the day we would see it happen with our own eyes.

But no sooner had the word been written on tablets than the blistering attacks began again, even worse than before. The devil never faced us off squarely; he always blindsided us. I will tell you something right now: He is sneaky, low-down, dirty, and mean, and in spiritual warfare, you can never expect him to play fair. He will destroy you in any way possible because there are no international rules of war in hell.

In April of 1991, my sister, who I'd just led to Christ, was diagnosed with ovarian cancer. She had a good husband and great kids, and she was being stricken with a possibly terminal disease, which put tremendous stress on our family as we tried to find a solution through prayer.

That June, charges were filed against our children's pastor for child molestation. It made all the local front pages, was reported in *USA Today,* on the TV news—everywhere. So anywhere you looked people were seeing a man from our church staff being taken away in handcuffs and shots of our building being linked to perversities of the most hideous kind. The worst part about it was that neither Debbie nor I had sinned, but we were having to take responsibility for failings within our church, and we had no way of seeing it coming.

The ten-year vision I had written down for all those wonderful things was by this time nearly in the garbage. Twenty-five acres? Right. Twenty-five-hundred-seat sanctuary? Not likely. Prayer chapel? Bible institute? Youth sanctuary? Citywide revival? All far-off dreams. I had so many other things to deal with that "vision" was the last thing on my agenda, and the overhead was buried somewhere deep in my desk. The vision itself was buried somewhere deep in my heart, out of sight and out of mind. I was working like crazy just to hold my own, preaching about healing, restoration, judgment, the presence of God, all the things that our church needed at the time to get through the mess. We were doing all we could to maintain present status—forget moving forward.

We lost a lot of people during that crisis, but an unexpected consequence was that the people who remained in the church bonded together almost like a family. We were unified, and we felt true to one another because we had stuck it out through the worst, and now there was loyalty to the church. As a result, the worship times became more glorious than ever before. I thank God for glimmers of light in dark situations. The worship services with those people were some of the few bright points in that time of struggle.

Then, as if those things were not enough, the attacks began again. The day after the first child molester was formally arrested, a second staff member, a maintenance man, was arrested for the same thing. Two days in a row. Again, there were front page headlines—"Second child molester arrested from same church." Television crews were all around our building, and our church's name was smeared all over town. The story headlined each news program that evening. There was not just one but two child molesters, both dragging our names into the mud. Debbie and I were deflated beyond comparison, and because the professional and personal lives of a minister and his family are knit so closely together, we could not simply escape from the pain in our work or home life. We were surrounded, and our morale was at rock bottom.

That following Easter, my sister died of ovarian cancer, even though we had prayed and believed with our whole hearts that she would be healed. I performed her funeral on Friday, and on Sunday, as part of our Easter program, I had to give a sermon on "The Miracles of Christ," how He healed the sick and raised the dead and gave sight to the blind. I could not help asking God why He had not healed my sister. Here we were having a healing service for others, and the prayers for our own household had not been answered.

I think it's true of all Christians that in times of trouble we turn to the Books of Psalms and Job. Job had it worse than all of us combined, and that makes us feel good. David suffered through danger after danger and heartache after heartache and still stayed true to God. The ages have shown that the encouragement in these books is rock solid, and as Christians we believe that God speaks to us personally through the same Scriptures. They are His vehicle for conveying hope to us. That was true in my life at that time.

A particular passage of Scripture that gave me strong comfort was in Psalm 139:5–6: "You have hedged me behind and before, And laid Your hand upon me. Such knowledge is too wonderful for me; It is high, I cannot attain it." When I read those words it was like God speaking directly to me: Glen, I have hedged you in behind and before, and laid my hand upon you. It's true: My knowledge is high, you cannot attain it. But the things I will do in your life are so wonderful that you simply cannot imagine them right now. So trust me, just trust me.

I did trust Him. I thanked Him for the word of comfort, which I needed so badly at that time, and we continued to press on doggedly through the haze of tribulation.

Chapter 14

An Offer to Make Money

I t was a standard day in the life of Frank Tanner: Go to work, put in the hours, come home, crack open a beer, and spend time with his daughter, the only person that made his life worth living. Frank tended not to think in terms of the big picture anymore. He kept his attention focused on the details, like the ones he looked for when reproducing the lithographs.

He had stopped comparing his life to the lives of his heroes. His life wasn't good and it wasn't bad. It just was, and Frank tried to accept that.

While he was working one day at the lithograph shop in Fremont, an old friend of Frank's, who had just been released from prison, dropped by in the middle of the day.

"Hey, Frank, how ya been?" Eddie asked. Frank cast him a wary glance. He didn't trust him and didn't want to be near him. The guy was bad luck.

"I'm okay. You out of prison?" he asked.

"Yeah, just got out a few weeks ago. Good to be free, I guess, though no one's there to serve your meals for you," he said and guffawed. It was clear he would have to readjust to civilian life.

"So, what can I help you with?" questioned Frank. Eddie gave him a furtive look, his hands in his pockets as if he were hiding something.

"I was wanting to know if anyone in the shop wants to help me print some money," he said.

"Yeah, right!" said one of Frank's fellow workers, laughing at the joke. With the high-tech lithograph machines they used in the shop, printing money would have been easy, but anyone in the industry knew how stiff the penalties were. Printing money was like touching the third rail on a subway track.

"That's a good one, huh," said Eddie, laughing. Apparently he had been joking, but an alarm had gone off in Frank's mind. This wasn't exactly Mr. Honesty he was talking to. He was slippery, like a snake, and Frank didn't doubt that he had been half serious.

His suspicions were confirmed later when Eddie cornered Frank and told him he really did want to print money.

"Look, I want to make up some counterfeit money, but I need your help," he said.

"No chance," said Frank, evading his friend. But Eddie followed him around the shop.

"It'll be easy, no one will get hurt," he said. "Just consider it a business transaction. I'd do it myself but I need an expert's help. You're an expert, aren't you, Frank?"

Frank stopped and took a breath. Eddie knew his weak spots.

"I'm still not going to do it," Frank said. Eddie tapped a coin on the counter and thought for a minute.

"Look, I'll come back later, after you have a chance to consider the offer," he said. "Then we'll talk. Maybe I'll even bring a little incentive."

"Don't bother," Frank said as Eddie went out the door, bells jangling, but the visit had gotten under Frank's skin.

The next day, Eddie came back and dropped an envelope containing several thousand dollars in cash on Frank's desk.

"I don't want this, Eddie. Get rid of it now," Frank said, but Eddie stood over him and grinned. "It's just one friend giving another some money. That's all. Don't feel indebted," he said. Frank stared at the envelope, then picked it up and shoved it at Eddie.

"It's yours, get it out of here," he said. Eddie dropped it back onto the desk and turned to leave. "Just hold onto it while you consider the offer," he said. Already the plan was in motion, and a small part of Frank felt the thrill of a good risk, a thrill he hadn't felt since crouching in his position on the baseball diamond or standing in front of thousands of cheering fans. He held onto the cash but refused to spend it, and he grew secretly afraid at what was happening. The situation was getting beyond his control, and little by little, Frank had allowed it to happen.

It wasn't long before two men came into the lithograph shop, men Frank had never seen before. He would learn later that they were members of the Chinese Mafia. They approached Frank and told him in no uncertain terms that if he didn't cooperate with their scheme to print counterfeit money they would put a bullet in his head, cut him up into tiny pieces, and put them in the bottom of the ocean. Frank, full of fear, thought of his daughter. He wanted to see her again. He didn't want her to lose her daddy. Against better judgment, and against the law, he agreed to print their money for them.

But by this time, the word had leaked to his fellow employees, who had contacted the Secret Service, who had bugged the entire shop with cameras and microphones. On January 7, 1995, agents busted the counterfeiting scheme, took over the lithograph shop, and seized the property. Frank, though he was under arrest by federal authorities, was relieved that he had been rescued from the web of fear, intimidation, and lawlessness.

"Thank you," he said as the agents handcuffed him. "Thank you for saving my life."

"You're going behind bars, buddy," the agent said.

"I don't care. At least I'll see my little girl again," Frank said as they led him to the car.

Chapter 15

New Highs,
New Lows

J avier Macias's search for a better high led him down the wrong road with the wrong crowd, threatening to turn him into another juvenile statistic on the evening news: A youth died of an overdose . . . was caught in petty burglary . . . was arrested as part of a gang sweep. If he had made the headlines, it wouldn't have been a story about how he had moved penniless from Guatemala and built an outstanding public reputation. It would have been a story of two orphans, left by their mother and father to fend for themselves in a strange new world. It would have been the story of one family after another dissolving into nothing. It would have been the story of two children clinging to each other through each wave of attack. The story of a young boy whose soul was dying in the promised land.

For the next two years Javier made good on his desire to explore the world of narcotics. He became a regular drug user, not just of illegal substances, but legal ones too. He followed his uncle's footsteps in taking up the bottle—an easy buzz that he and his friends could enjoy on the weekends or at parties where the beer, wine, and liquor flowed freely. He took up cigarettes, because they made him look cool, made him feel adult, and declared his independence from his aunt. He used more and more marijuana—because it took more to get him high. Then he graduated to the hardest stuff on the market, mainly crank. He experimented with anything available, anything that his friends were doing, and no one was there to stop him.

His aunt, since being single again, had been working all hours of the day just to earn enough for the children and herself. She gave them the clothes they needed, paid for their schoolbooks, bought them backpacks, games, and bicycles. But she didn't give them the attention they wanted or the discipline they needed. She had rescued them from certain disaster in the orphanage, but her own life had taken one bad turn after another, leaving her in a circumstance she had never dreamed of. She gave the children everything they needed, but being expected to love and care for them when she hadn't even recovered from her own loss was too much.

In the absence of a father or an uncle, Javier became the man of the house, barely a teenager himself. There was a strong streak of goodness in him, and at times he filled the role perfectly, tending to things his aunt didn't have time for, being sure his sister got off to school, and keeping a good home like an adult would have done. But there were also the bad times. He rebelled against his aunt's authority, which he felt she hadn't earned. He yelled back at her during extended arguments where they blamed each other for the mess they were in. When he couldn't win, he sulked in his room or left the house and spent the night with a friend.

And there were always the drugs to turn to.

The accumulated bitterness of his early childhood welled up inside him and made him constantly angry. He could not see a way out of the anger, so he used more drugs, hung around with the gangs in his neighborhood, and slept around with some of the girls from his school. He only dabbled in crime, where his friends were often unruly and without conscience, but they dragged his life lower and lower, clouding the expectations he had once had about having a good career and family. Javier's ambition for better things, evident from the time he was a small boy, was being denied, undermined, and forgotten. The only civilizing factor in his life was his little sister, who depended on him as her only real family. They were close to one another, and Javier felt a certain responsibility for making sure she was ready for school, feeding her, and acting as her disciplinarian. But more often he felt bitter that he was forced into the role of a father at a time when he would have given anything for a father himself.

Javier's whole life reflected his new dropout attitude. His relationship with his aunt was virtually nonexistent. They stayed on separate tracks when they were home together, which was better than fighting, Javier had decided. In school, he had let everything go and was getting straight F's, even in physical education. When he was in class he did more to disrupt the lesson than he did to learn anything. At times, his teachers wished he hadn't come to class at all, though they grieved the loss of yet another teenage boy.

Javier was charting an early course to nowhere, that nameless, hopeless place where society dumped its failures. It was all the more pitiful because of the spark he knew was inside of him, the glimmer of light in his personality that said he had the goods to make something of himself, despite his circumstances. But with every puff on a cigarette or a joint and every drink from the bottle, the light came closer and closer to going out.

Chapter **16**

The Louisiana-Modesto Connection

I n 1993 I was still traveling and speaking on occasion as I always did, getting out around the country during the week, away from Baton Rouge, and those miniretreats helped me weather the storms at home. Getting an outside perspective encouraged me. It seemed to lift the burden for a while, and I tried to bring that encouragement home, but Debbie, unfortunately, didn't have the luxury of getting out as much as I did so she was in the thick of it for longer periods of time.

It was when I was speaking at the Oregon youth convention that I met pastor Joe Wright of Calvary Temple in Modesto, California, who had come to Oregon with the specific purpose of talking to me. Joe Wright was a veteran pastor in the Assemblies of God, a real war hero in the battle for God's kingdom, and he had pastored Calvary Temple for many years. A series of things had happened without my knowledge that led him to seek me out at the youth convention. Many years earlier, when I was at Swaggart Ministries, two of his sons had attended Jimmy Swaggart Bible College, studied youth ministry in my classes, and their own ministries had been profoundly enriched by my own. His daughter and son-in-law had flown out for one of our youth ministry conferences and had heard me speak. Further, one of his staff members had also come out to Louisiana for a conference we did, so in all there were five people Wright knew—four of them in his family—who had been affected by my ministry. I had never been to Modesto, but Modesto sure had been to Baton Rouge.

While I was going through 1988 and its five-year aftermath, Joe Wright had been climbing toward retirement age. His family had been asking him who he was thinking about getting to replace him, but he didn't have an answer. Then his children suggested my name, in fact, they kept on suggesting my name for three years, which is why Joe Wright finally came to Portland, Oregon, looking for me.

"Brother Glen, I'm Joe Wright from Calvary Temple in Modesto, California," he said as he approached me after one of the meetings. We greeted one another, and he asked if I would come down and speak at one of his family camps in California. I told him I would love to, and then he said there was something else he wanted to talk to me about.

"You know, I am sixty-five years old and am going to be retiring here pretty soon," he said.

"That is great," I said. "What are you going to do?"

"Well, I'll get my old RV and travel around some."

"How about your church?"

"Well, I have been praying about it, and I feel like God has told me you are supposed to take it."

I was momentarily stunned. We had briefly met before and here he was asking me to lead his congregation. A number of thoughts rushed through my head as I tried to maintain my composure. *Me? Take his church? A church I know nothing about?* In some no-name town, in California of all places? I could not see the Lord working in this at all and was more than a little skeptical. Not wanting to be rude, I made some light remarks and tried to deflect the issue.

"Tell me about your church, Joe," I said.

"Well," he said, "we have got twenty-five acres and a twenty-five-hundred-seat sanctuary. We have got a beautiful prayer chapel and a youth sanctuary that seats 550. Oh, and you would be president of the Bible institute to train youth ministers, because I know that is your heart . . . "

My heart had already stopped beating and I was nearly floored. All I could do was stand there looking at him. In one sentence he had read my vision overhead—the one I had written down three years earlier, the one I had all but forgotten about while getting hit by wave after wave of enemy attacks, the one I had lost under a pile of broken dreams. Joe Wright didn't know it, but he had spoken words that grabbed my attention; more than that, they virtually took me by the lapels and lifted me off my feet.

Still a little stunned, I told him that we should talk more about it later and put it to prayer. When I got back to my hotel room I knelt right down and began to pray.

"Lord," I said, "I don't understand what you are telling me. Here I am in a church in Baton Rouge that seems to be just getting its legs back, things are working, the people are gelling, the staff is solid and dependable. I feel like we have brought it through the bad times and that we have remained faithful, but now there is a pull in a new direction."

Glen, the Lord told me in response, *I gave you a vision, but I never told you to build those things. I wanted to give them to you. I want you to go there to Modesto, California, and fill that church.*

I went back to Louisiana, and for the next few months our church prospered even more. There was a new robustness in the congregation, and Debbie and I became even more confused because we had Modesto in our spirits, even as the church in Baton Rouge was just coming into its own as a vibrant place of worship.

I knew God was leading us west, but I kept getting mixed signals, and because I am of imperfect faith I needed confirmations from God. I need not have worried, because He was right there to give them to me.

We decided to make an exploratory trip to Modesto to preach on a Sunday. We got to see the facilities there, and they lived up to our dream: a beautiful state-of-the-art sanctuary, a gorgeous white-water fountain out front, tree-lined walkways, a stained-glass prayer chapel, and separate buildings for the elementary school, youth meetings, and Bible institute. Debbie and I were more than excited because the Lord was confirming the word He had planted in our hearts. He was showing us with our own eyes the beginning of the vision He had given to us those many years ago.

That Sunday I preached straight and hard, and, to be honest, I was not actively looking for a job because I already had one back in Baton Rouge. I was not trying to impress anybody with my "pastoral qualities," and I didn't change a thing about myself—not my southern accent or my evangelistic fire. I gave them the undiluted Glen Berteau because I was looking for that absolute confirmation that I was the guy they wanted. In a way, I was setting out a fleece—and their response was incredible. Not only did they give us a standing ovation before I had even said a word, but people filled the altars that night to pray for their city. I could see by their prayers and their actions that the people were hungry for a move of God, and I knew that together, we could go places in reaching that foreign land, the Central Valley.

We returned to Louisiana with the firm belief that God was moving us forward into a new chapter of our lives, but then I began to have apprehensions about leaving the church in Baton Rouge, which are difficult to explain in terms of hard, cold logic. I had grown attached to the church, and it had been our goal to show them integrity and stability in the pulpit. I simply did not want them to feel ripped off again, and I thought the church might crumble without strong leadership, that leaving the people would be disillusioning. I felt like parents feel when the time comes to let one of their children walk on his own. But letting go is a necessary part of the growth process for both the parent and the child, and to dispel those notions, God did something He had never done before: He woke me up in the middle of the night with an answer. Now, as a minister, I know a lot of people who get words from the Lord in the middle of the night, but it had never happened to me before. He generally lets me sleep. But on this night He woke me up at 2:30 A.M. and said, *Let the church go, it can make it. You have put the ministers in place, do not take any of them with you. Leave them there to keep the church strong, but you need to go. You have stayed the time that I wanted you to, and now you are released. Go fill that church in Modesto.*

That was the last confirmation we needed, so Debbie and I prepared our family to make the break from Louisiana, and then we told our church what the Lord was doing in our ministry and that it was time for us to leave. From that point on the Lord began to bring us into His understanding of what had happened in our lives. We knew we had been through five years of spiritual warfare—hand-to-hand combat with the devil, a jungle war with land mines, camouflaged snipers, and relentless air attacks on our family and church. We had gone through the flames and come out alive, and now we were trained in spiritual battle. We were smart and tough and strong, seasoned veterans in the war for souls. We had taken every hit possible, but we had held the line, and now it was our turn—the tide of battle was changing and we were going on the offensive.

The Bible says in the Book of Joel, "I will restore to you the years that the swarming locust has eaten" (2:25). I had come through a time when it seemed like the locusts had eaten everything worth having, and I felt like I was left with nothing but fields of stubble. I felt like we were entering a time when the past five years would be restored to us. We had dropped back; we had submitted to the Lord; and we knew in our hearts that God was going to bless us a hundredfold, just like He said He would bless those who forsook everything, father and mother, brother and sister, lands and houses, for the gospel.

Never had we felt such a spirit of expectation than when we were preparing to move to Modesto. The Lord made it abundantly clear to us that He was going to do something amazing, something we would have to see to believe. He was blowing on the embers in my heart, and they were beginning to glow again, first a hint of orange beneath the ashes and then a fierce red, casting away all doubts and fears. The fire, the vision, was being reignited. We were ready for the promises of God to burst into flames.

Chapter **17**

Headed for Modesto

Modesto, California, is a city where the sun rises on misty peach orchards, sprawling vineyards, and thousand-acre industrial farms, and the temperature never seems to dip below forty degrees Fahrenheit. If ever God had demonstrated His bounty on earth, it is in California, where you barely have to wet the ground to bring forth crops of every shape and color.

That's why, as we loaded up a big moving van with everything we owned—tables, appliances, beds, shelves, couches, children—and headed for Modesto in 1993, two words defined our spirit: *fruitfulness* and *increase.* Here we were, moving to the most fertile and abundant agricultural area in the world, but our hunger was for more than food. We knew that we were going to see not only a harvest of fruit and vegetables, but a harvest of souls, a harvest that would come on time, in God's season.

In the meantime, there were a lot of questions still unanswered, and we had some cultural readjusting to do. Our life was full of unknowns, beginning with the great, yawning space between Louisiana and California. It's a good thing that Debbie and I don't predicate our actions on the peace of God, because we have often faced very unpeaceful situations. What God demands of us is obedience, even though people often fear that God has abandoned them because they don't feel the peace. We pray and pray and pray for the peace, without examining our own attitude and asking ourselves, *Am I being obedient to God?* Peace comes through obedience. I imagine Abraham didn't have much peace when he was taking his son up the mountain to sacrifice him, but he had obedience, and the answer to his situation—the answer that would provide peace—came through that. It is too easy for us to value the peace of God over obedience to Him.

Moving to Modesto was one of those unpeaceful situations, because we were leaving behind all that we knew: Our kids were leaving their friends; we were leaving a church that had become like family to us; we were leaving our people, our region, our culture. To further complicate things, when we got to Modesto we could not find a house. Our moving van, full of Louisiana furniture, was parked in the middle of a California parking lot, and our family had no place to go. But we knew we were being obedient; we knew we had been called to participate in a work of God; that gave us a measure of contentment through the insecurity. Soon we found a place to stay temporarily, and then we found a home we could buy and settle in permanently. That did a lot for establishing our presence in the area, because up to that point we had felt more or less like drifters in the California winds.

Moving across the country can sometimes be like moving to another country. As southerners, we had the typical view of California as a place for crazies, wackos, and fringe cultures—the place that spawned the hippie movement and the peace and love generation. In my mind, the whole state was one big Berkeley and I wondered how we would relate with everybody, considering that the only hippie in the South was the one who was passing through. To my great surprise, the people were not all hippies; on the contrary, they were normal—and they were friendly! In fact, they were some of the friendliest people I had ever met anywhere in the U.S.

The people from Calvary Temple were so gracious and kind when we arrived that it gave us a wonderful first impression of our new home and made us feel instantly like we belonged. They helped us move our things into our new home, then they brought fruit for us— not fruit baskets, you understand, but fruit right off the trees. Peaches in big wooden crates with the dirt still on them, paper bags full of almonds, apples, oranges, anything that grew. This stuff was fresh and plump and bursting with flavor. Between the paradise weather and the bounty of fresh fruit, we felt like we were in heaven.

Aside from the people there were a number of other surprises awaiting us in California. When we first got there, everyone kept referring to "the Valley." "Here in the Central Valley it can get pretty hot in the summer . . ." "Just drive up the valley a ways . . ." "He lives in the North Valley . . ." It didn't make much sense, because where I am from, a valley means the place where two mountains come together, and maybe there is a river meandering through, a log cabin with smoke drifting out of the chimney, horses in a field, and so forth.

But in California—where everything is bigger—*valley* means a vast, fertile, agricultural plain, nothing like the valleys I had envisioned. Modesto sits in the middle of the great San Joaquin Valley, which runs north and south and makes up the heart of California. It is over a hundred miles in width, sits between two great mountain ranges, and is so wide that from the floor of the valley you can't even see both ranges at one time. My family had to go through a quick geography lesson just to acquaint ourselves with local news jargon: "It'll be a hot, dry day in the Central Valley today, now let's look at our average rainfall numbers . . ."

We also were not accustomed to such a variety of terrain in one state. In Louisiana, folks who wanted to hang around in the hills had to take a trip up to the Smokey Mountains in Tennessee, and folks who wanted to take a beach vacation had to trundle off to Florida—there were not really any alternatives. But in California we were within driving distance of a whole range of beaches, major urban centers like San Francisco and Los Angeles, a number of impressive and striking mountain ranges, lakes, rivers, camping spots, ski resorts, deserts—any type of geography you could imagine. The fact that we could make a day trip to these places and sleep in our own beds at night was a wonder to us.

One further question I had about our new home region when we first arrived was, for lack of a more delicate way to put it, How in the world do you make a living with fruit? I had grown up and lived mostly in Texas and Louisiana, where people made their money in oil. I was used to industries where workers manufactured things or drilled for them or refined them. Out here, people were growing things—grapes, almonds, walnuts, peaches, apples, apricots, oranges, asparagus, artichokes, onions, garlic, rice, tomatoes—our new home county was the breadbasket of the world. But the idea of making money on something that grew out of the ground (and would probably do so on its own anyway) was still hard for me to conceive of, even if they did it in great quantities like most farmers had to to make a living. Only gradually did I learn the amount of hard work it takes to produce a good crop every year, and the more I learned and observed California's native industries, the more I admired those who worked the land and made their money in the soil—and, of course, appreciated the results.

California is so well-known as the fresh produce state that it overshadows almost everything else. Modesto is best known for being the place where E & J Gallo Winery was founded and headquartered, so when I first told people I had moved to Modesto, Gallo was the only thing I knew that would help them distinguish our city from all the rest.

"Modesto? Where in the world is Modesto?"

"Ever heard of Gallo winery?"

"Sure."

"Well, their home office is there."

"Ohhhh . . . "

But I soon grew tired of having to use Gallo as a distinguishing feature. I wanted Modesto to be known for something greater. "We need some new wine," I said. "When people think of Modesto I want them to think of the wine of the Spirit that was poured out in our community."

I believed that we would see some new wine and give our city a new reputation, and so we began to acquaint ourselves with the area, exploring different neighborhoods and avenues. As I drove around exploring the place, I noticed that most of the time I saw only groves of trees, fields of crops, scattered neighborhoods, country houses, schools, and so on; the more I drove, the more confused I became. We were supposed to be living in the city of Modesto, so where was the city? All I could see were subdivisions, fruit orchards, and vineyards—no real buildings or "downtowns." There didn't seem to be a center to anything, and it was somewhat disorienting.

My definition of city had to change to fit the new circumstance because this was an agricultural society—flat, spread out, leafy, dusty, and hot. I was accustomed to a different landscape: refineries belching smoke on the horizon, acres of impassable and mysterious swamps and marshland, and concentrated cities with big buildings and skylines. Where I lived, the urban centers took up a lot less room; they tended to go up rather than out. California cities were different— they built out rather than up because they have a lot of room to work with. As a result, Modesto looked like a small town wherever I went. I wrongly assumed that there must not be that many people there, that is, until someone informed me that over two-hundred-fifty thousand people lived in the Modesto area. *A quarter of a million people!* I thought. *Where are they hiding?*

But in my mind, I was thrilled, for I had always believed that such a place would be perfect for reaching the lost. Unlike a big city, it was not trampled down by evangelists. Big cities, like New York or Atlanta, tended to be hot spots for crusades, and if they didn't work on one side of town you could always go try your luck on the other. Every outreach tried to "out-big" the other, and urban dwellers became somewhat jaded to the appeals to their soul.

But a place like Modesto was different. It had the population of a substantial urban center, but it had a small-town feel. It was large enough to support a major move of God and small enough that every corner would know about it. The people were not jaded. Their city had been preserved from the crisscross pattern of traveling "revivalists."

The city was ripe and ready for something great to happen. The harvest would come, and as we settled into our new home, I knew that this was the platform God had intended for us, the place to see the vision fulfilled. It was only a matter of when and how. But if there was one thing I had learned about the ministry, it was that God's timing is perfect . . . even in the midst of disaster.

Chapter 18

Cajun in a Modesto Pulpit

With a small amount of trepidation and a large dose of enthusiasm, Debbie and I set about preparing ourselves to take the helm at Calvary Temple in Modesto and use it as a center of ministry for reaching the whole city. For six months Joe Wright remained as pastor, and I submitted to his leadership as his long tenure wound to an end. In January 1994 I became senior pastor, and when we first were installed, it was like a new wind had blown into the church. People all over town were talking about the Cajun from the swamps with the funny accent who had taken over the pulpit at Calvary.

I wanted to establish right away that we were there for a purpose, and so the first message I preached to the church was the vision of three years earlier that I had recorded on the overhead transparency, the one that I had all but forgotten as God was breaking us to pieces—

the vision I had lost, but which God had renewed. I spoke on Habakkuk 2:2–3: "'Write the vision And make it plain on tablets, That he may run who reads it. For the vision is yet for an appointed time; But at the end it will speak, and it will not lie. Though it tarries, wait for it; Because it will surely come, It will not tarry.'"

As confirmation that God had brought Debbie and me there for a purpose, I showed them the original overhead on which I had written down the vision. He had a vision for us. We had waited for it until the appointed time, and just as He had promised, the vision was not over-due one single day. He had described their church to a guy in Baton Rouge who had never even heard of Modesto, then He had moved me two thousand miles from my home. Clearly, the Lord had a vision for the city, and we, the church, were going to be a part of it.

Now, at such times of transition, one of the first things a church member wants to know is how well the new man preaches. That is a pretty easy judgment to make: Either he can or he can't.

But though most of the contact between pastor and congregation takes place for a few hours on Sunday, the majority of a pastor's time is not spent preaching, it's spent doing the mundane, day-to-day things that make a church successful: making decisions about money, discipling staff members, approving building projects, planning for the future, and so on. In this area it takes some time to demonstrate trustworthiness. The people have to see your leadership in action, and they have to trust you to take care of the details before they will listen to the vision you have for the church. Just as pilots and astronauts are tested in a thousand different ways before they are allowed to fly their aircraft, so a pastor gets put through a series of tests by his people that either confirms or denies his ability to navigate. When they see that he is comfortable in the cockpit and knows what all the switches and buttons are for, then they let him take off. Only then will they be receptive to his vision, because they trust his judgment.

In our first few months at Calvary, I was doing two things at once: introducing our vision to the church and demonstrating my ability to lead. Debbie and I were believing for revival because God had plant-

94

ed the seed in our spirits. We didn't know when or how or in what form it would come, but we knew it would come. Because we knew it would come, the Lord impressed upon my heart the need to have a good staff of ministers ready when it did come. To change the analogy, I was the church's new quarterback, and I needed a championship team. I needed a staff of pros—in football they call them "high draft choices"—men and women who are proficient at their jobs and can, in simple terms, get the job done right. I believed we were going to have to handle a great move of God, probably beyond what most of us had seen. I wanted excellence in place before it happened.

But it was important to me that we not have a staff full of "stars," because most championship teams don't have stars. I knew from my football days that a good team is made up of team players, not one or two outstanding individuals. People on our staff were going to have to give up their individual approach—"God using me"—and take on a team approach—"God using us."

There were growing pains on the church staff as a result of the change in leadership, not severe ones, but growing pains nonetheless. When I began creating new positions, eliminating old ones, and replacing some people, the response was sometimes puzzled and a little touchy. I knew what was crossing some people's minds: *What is he doing? Did he not like things the way they were? Where is he going with all of this?*

What I was doing, in fact, was building a tight, family-like unit: putting people in positions that best suited their talents, and, therefore, adding to their confidence. Furthermore, I wanted people to feel like they were on the team and on the team for good. Once we had established the starting lineup, that was it—no more cuts, no fear of being canned if they messed up. I wanted each staff member to know that I was committed to him or her even in their failings, because loyalty is such a big part of good discipleship. If they did something wrong, we would sit down and talk about it, but there was no air of job insecurity in the office. There was a happiness and an openness. I had chosen them; they had chosen me; and we were married.

The first thing I did as the financial leader of the church was to step out in faith in the area of finances. For a number of years the church budget had been tight. They had been making it, but just barely. People had gotten used to functioning on a lean bank account and were on a perpetual diet. There is nothing intrinsically wrong with this—most churches in America are the same way—but I believe that in this generation the Lord is calling us to a greater work, not just at our church but at every church, and that greater work will require growth in the area of money. I believe that the Lord intends to supply the added resources to His church to help fulfill His vision.

I began believing for a greater monthly income for the church to work with, not just greater by a few thousand dollars, but substantially greater. I told the church board I was believing for an expanded budget of such-and-such amount every month. All but a few of them thought I was crazy; I could see it in their eyes. But for every month since that time we have exceeded my "faith estimate."

The Lord provides when His people have faith, if only they will have faith. When the people believe in one area, they begin to believe in all the others as well, so that the church begins to grow and prosper and the faith muscle becomes strong. Such is the nature of revival: If you do not work out for it, you will never be able to handle it when it comes, and if you do not believe for the small things to happen, the big things never will.

Chapter 19

The Spirit
at Cagney's Bar

Lane had been acting strange.

"You ought to go with me sometime, Doug. The people are good, and the pastor's got fire," Lane said.

Great, Doug thought. *Lane's going to ruin another fine afternoon with his gospel sales pitch.*

"Look, ask some of the other guys. You know I mean it: I ain't going. I don't have the time, and if I did I wouldn't waste it on church," Doug said, leaning against the bar.

"Well, someday you'll go with me, and I'll keep praying for you," Lane said as he refilled Doug's drink. Doug snorted, something he'd been doing ever since Lane began bringing it up. But the snort was much less hearty and spontaneous than it had been at the beginning. Now he did it to reiterate what he thought of Lane's latest fad.

Ever since Lane's wife had convinced him to go to a local church, he hadn't been his usual self. In fact, he hadn't been drinking, or if he had, nobody else in the bar knew it. He just kept talking about the "Spirit"—"Spirit" this and "Jesus" that, and "you need the Lord," and so on and so forth.

Doug was sick of hearing about it. He wanted to drink in peace, drive his truck in peace, and go home to sleep off whatever misery remained. As long as he paid off the seven hundred dollar bar bill that he accumulated each month, everything was okay.

But Lane kept at it. He would lean back against the counter lined with liquor bottles and talk about "that church" until the patrons begged him to shut up. Worse than that he began recruiting some of the guys to go with him. As close-knit as they were, they tended to go in groups, just to satisfy Lane.

Then something even stranger started happening: When they came back from the church service, Doug would hear about his various friends going forward to accept God and making a change in their lives. Doug laughed and laughed at them, mocking their weakheartedness, wondering aloud how a church could make them do something so stupid.

But after a few weeks, he couldn't ignore it anymore, and when they brought it up he felt a stab of fear in his heart. Maybe they would stop coming to the bar. Maybe the bar would close down. Maybe Doug would be abandoned again.

Lane Cagney, the owner of the bar, wasn't going back to his old ways like Doug had expected. Doug knew Lane's wife was a holy roller, and she always told Lane she was praying for him—to Doug, prayer was a joke, a concession—but when Lane himself confessed that her prayers had worked and that now he prayed too, it was too much. Doug saw Lane go from being a charter member of the Cagney's bar gang—a rowdy, hard-living bunch with nothing more than bad attitudes to their credit—to a man filled with the Holy Spirit, thanks in large part to prayer on the part of his wife and her fanatical church friends.

Doug didn't care if his friends were wimps, he wouldn't go even if he were the last holdout. He eyed Lane over the lip of his glass. Lane was whistling a song Doug had never heard; it certainly wasn't on the jukebox.

"What's that song?" he demanded after a few minutes.

"A chorus we sing at church," Lane said. Doug slammed his glass down, slid off the bar and headed out the door.

"You know I'll be back in here tomorrow, but for now I'm sick of you preaching at me," Doug said. Lane just smiled.

On his way home Doug tried to sort it out. He didn't want anything else; everything he had ever wished for had eluded him, and he'd been burned instead. He had his apartment, his job, and his bar bill, and those things made him happy. Anyone who told him otherwise—including his best friend—was walking into territory that was off-limits.

Chapter 20

From Stockton to Modesto

Tammy Jones finally had a chance to start over, free from the domination of her childhood tormentor and the mother who sold Tammy out for her own addictions. Within six months after moving to Stockton she had met Kyle, a slight man with quiet resolve and a working man's dedication. He was the man who would become her first husband. Unlike the other men she'd known, he was kind to her and treated her with love and respect. In 1985 they married and had their first child together.

But old habits remained. Tammy was still heavily addicted to heroin, and consequently a regular thief in local clothing and grocery stores. Tutored in criminal behavior, she stole clothing to return it for its cash value. Kyle worked ten to twelve hours a day, seven days a week, to keep up Tammy's drug habit and to keep her from "ripping and running" items from local stores. Still, a ray of hope had shined into her life. She had a husband who loved her and would provide for her, and they were starting a family. They had a house and a car. Her life was no longer as chaotic as it used to be; she no longer had to wonder where their next meal would come from, didn't have to be looking over her shoulder for the police all the time. For the first time, Tammy began to feel like she had firm ground to stand on, and that made her life worthwhile.

Then 1986 struck. On January 1, Tammy's and Kyle's one-year anniversary, their infant baby boy died of bronchial pneumonia. Eight months later, Tammy's seven-year-old son, Jack, accidentally hanged himself. There was no warning for their deaths. Once again, evil had made its ugly presence known in her life, stripping her of the only people she truly loved.

These tragedies ushered in Tammy's worst heroin-using period. Her love for her children had kept her holding on to a life ragged with fear and abuse. Now two of them were gone—only five-year-old Earl remained—and once again, she felt she was over the edge. She didn't want her life anymore and she tried to end it by doing more and more drugs in heavier doses, but her body wouldn't die, no matter how much dope she put into her veins. One night she swallowed 160 Valium, drank a fifth of whiskey, and still woke up the next morning— disappointed to be alive.

In the year that followed, Tammy was arrested for a number of crimes: drug possession, petty theft, drug purchase and sale. She normally would have been more cautious because of her children, but only one wasn't enough for a guardrail for her behavior. She still didn't stop using drugs or stealing clothing and food, and each arrest brought her closer and closer to a permanent prison sentence.

Over the next four years, tragedy struck regularly in the Jones family. Kyle's brother died in 1987. His mother died in 1988. Tammy's mother died in 1989, and her stepfather died in 1990. Most tragic of all, by the time her mother died, Tammy had landed herself in the county jail again—this time for nearly a year.

The charge was drug possession, hardly a major infraction, but enough to put her out of circulation. Tammy had been to jail several times before on minor charges, but the corrections system was lost on her. She had come to see jail as a vacation spot where she had a bed to sleep in, free meals, security—a good time for rest and relaxation before returning to the outside. Plus, she knew all the other inmates. They were her drug clients and fellow users.

The county jail may as well have been a country club.

But the long stay left her son, Earl, without a mother. Kyle was faithful to the family and brought Earl to visit Tammy every weekend, but the separation—and the fact that it was her fault—drove Tammy to a point of decision: She had to either function as a mother or as a drug addict. She knew from example that the two lifestyles were incompatible. Her husband and son were being faithful to her, but she was not being faithful to them with her actions, and she felt it was time to change all of that. She mustered her resolve and decided to kick her drug habit and live straight.

Admitting that she was wrong and trying to change her life meant showing weaknesses that she'd had to hide since she was a little girl. It forced her to let her defenses down—the defenses that had kept her from going crazy in each successive, life-wrecking situation. In her hardened way of life, strength had always been of capital importance: You didn't show people your real self. You put up a tough exterior in order to survive. Now she had to reverse that process and come out of her shell to address who she was as a person.

In jail, she attended a few church services put on by an outreach ministry and was given a Bible. She came out of incarceration drug free, but the Bible was quickly put away among storage boxes and forgotten. The reunited family hoped to make a new start and move to a house in a place called Modesto, where Kyle was pretty sure he could get employment. But the neighborhood was rougher than anything Tammy had ever seen, even in jail. Earl was befriended by gang members, who offered him drugs, and Tammy could not bear to see her own cycle of addiction repeat itself in Earl's life.

After she witnessed a gang-related murder right across the street from her home and testified in a county court, their moving plans were accelerated. They feared retaliation by gang members, and the family took what they had and got out as quickly as they could. In their new house, across town in a better neighborhood, Tammy hoped for an end to her brutal past. Modesto would prove either her saving grace or her last battle, because without a new direction, Tammy wasn't sure she wanted to go on.

Chapter 21

Faith for Revival

aith in our church began to have growth spurts, not just in the area of finances, but in every other area as well. We were building the vision of seeing citywide revival together. But as every visionary knows, people don't just line up behind you because you are saying something that gets their blood pumping. There is a time of persuasion that comes before the time of complete unity. It's up to a leader both to lead and to draw people into the vision God has given him.

The early days of such a situation can sometimes be lonely. I remember feeling at one point that the things I was saying to the staff and the congregation were not catching on. I wanted them to think in new ways, so I had to show them why those new ways were better, right, and God-ordained. During transition, it is up to the visionary to trust the vision God has given him and believe that the people will follow. In the beginning, at times I felt like I was standing alone; on the other hand, I never doubted that in the end we would all be unified around the same vision.

I knew it was my responsibility to communicate the vision in order that the people could embrace it when they had seen it. I had an old mentality—I learned it in football—that you either produce results or quit talking. I had been to conferences and meetings and seminars and get-togethers where people talked on and on about what ought to be done to reach souls. The problem was, they could not point to any results. One passage of Scripture dealing with just this phenomenon hit me one day as a young man. Paul was encouraging the Philippians: "The things which you learned and received and saw in me, these do" (4:9).

I saw three steps in Paul's command: verbalization, visualization, and manifestation. We spend all of our efforts in Bible college and elsewhere "learning" and "receiving" and "hearing," because we think, *If I can become a better communicator and preacher, these great and powerful things will come to pass.*

To a certain extent that is true, but we tend to miss the visual demonstration of power. Paul said to follow the example of what they had seen him do. We need the visual demonstration of everything we believe in so that it can be manifested. We need leaders who will not shy away from believing in God's magnificent promises but who will stand in the pulpit and declare them so that the church can see someone of faith in action.

I came to realize that it is the responsibility of pastors and evangelists to demonstrate the vision, to stand up and shout it with eyes full of belief, so that their followers know what to do. I knew that before we could have a churchwide and citywide manifestation of power, the church needed to see in its own leadership a demonstration of power and a living faith. The church sees it, for example, in the power of believing in a larger budget and then meeting that goal. They see it in the power of believing that the right person will come along for a particular position at the church, and waiting for that person—not giving in to second best—and finally having that person arrive to demonstrate a new brand of excellence in music or pastoring that the church has never seen before. I believe the reason Paul told the Philippians to emulate what was seen in him was because power comes from seeing. It dominates our other senses, and the impression we get from a picture cannot be erased. We can talk until we're hoarse, and people may or may not hear and respond, but to see is to believe.

From the time I was a young man, I applied that bit of football wisdom (taken from Paul in his letter to the Philippians) to my own life. "Put up or shut up"—put it into practice or stop talking about it. I prayed, "Lord, give me a ministry that people can see. I don't want to talk about it, because I have nothing else to add to Your promises. Show people a manifestation of Your glory, and give me something I can point to."

When we were in Baton Rouge doing all of our leadership conferences, I would stand on the stage and tell youth leaders from around the country about our youth ministry, how many youth we had coming, how many we were following up with each week, about all the great things the Lord was doing in our ministry. They would nod and agree with me, but I knew it was not getting into their heads. From my words alone they could not visualize it, so I always invited them to come see for themselves.

When they did come, they sat in our meetings, amazed at what was going on around them. They would see everything I had told them about, and afterwards they would say, "Glen, I could not have believed this if I had not seen it. I heard you talk about it, but it just didn't hit home." I didn't want to just preach to the people at Calvary Temple on the revivals of the past or what had happened overseas in Africa or India with millions saved in tent crusades. Those things were wonderful, but what was happening here in America? What was happening among our people that we could see? I wanted a manifestation of power in Modesto, a real modern-day revival, a California earthquake that would shake our community and send them running to the Lord's side. I wanted the people in my church to know that I did not just think big, that I stuck with the vision until the big things happened.

A verse in Habakkuk (3:2) had been highlighted in my Bible for years: "O Lord, revive thy work in the midst of the years, in the midst of the years make [it] known" (KJV). In other words, do it again, Lord. Give us revival! That was the cry of my spirit. Do not allow us to remain dry in Your presence, but give us new wine; Lord, quench our thirst for a move of the Spirit. Do it again, Lord! Do it today like You did it back then; help us to stop pointing at the past and start pointing to the future.

The Lord was preparing to do it again, right there in Modesto, because a church was believing that He would. But no matter how much we prayed and believed that it would happen, what He had in store for us was far beyond what any one of us could have imagined. It would bring us to heights we didn't know possible, allowing us to look down on the valleys of our lives and see that they had a purpose, a part to play in the divine plan. For even the worst times in life gain new meaning when we see them through eternal eyes—though sometimes with our limited human vision, when we are going through the pain of the present, seeing God's plan seems next to impossible.

Chapter **22**

Preparing for Revival

One of the first things I did after becoming pastor was to schedule the drama "Heaven's Gates & Hell's Flames" for the following January. I had never seen the drama before, but other pastors had told me it was a powerful outreach tool. So I called Rudy Krulik at Reality Outreach in Canada and told him we wanted to host the drama. He explained a bit how it worked.

I found out that "Heaven's Gates & Hell's Flames" is much more than a drama or a play, though that is how it is commonly referred to. It is, in fact, a ministry to the local church, intended not just to impress people, but to draw them into a relationship with Christ. Reality Outreach, which has been doing dramas for sixteen years and now supports twenty-two teams worldwide, sends a husband and wife team to the church that is hosting the drama three days before it is to begin. The team oversees the construction of a set, provides the script and lighting and music directions, and trains all of the church volunteers in their parts. It's really incredible what they do: putting together a powerful hour-long play with actors and an impressive stage in only two and a half days.

The drama itself begins in darkness and then spotlights Jesus as He comes down the aisle carrying the cross. There are all sorts of sound effects and musical accompaniments as He climbs the stage, is crucified, dies, and then goes to hell where he drags the devil out (wearing a black outfit with his face painted black and red) and tears away the keys to hell from him once and for all. Then Jesus ascends the stairs into heaven amidst a chorus of angels and the "Hallelujah Chorus," and the ascendancy of Christ is established.

From there the play unfolds in a series of short, real-life vignettes, depicting people in everyday situations who make a choice to accept or reject Christ. After their decisions, each one dies suddenly and is taken to the gates of heaven to stand before heavenly hosts and wait to hear whether his or her name is in the Lamb's Book of Life. For those who have chosen Christ, it is a triumphant moment: The angels smile and Jesus comes out to welcome them into heaven, accompanying them through the gates as the "Hallelujah Chorus" fills the air. For those who don't know Christ, it's a terrifying moment when the angel tells them their names are not in the Book of Life, and the devil and his demons come to drag them away amidst horrible strobing red lights and cacophonous sound effects.

One scene shows two construction workers on lunch break as they shoot the breeze, gradually turning to serious topics, which allows one to share his faith in the gospel with the other. After a lot of bantering, the unsaved worker is led to the Lord just before a wall falls and kills them both, before they can even get to their sandwiches. They awaken to find themselves in a new place, at the foot of heaven's gates. They both find that their names are in the Book of Life and are given passage into heaven, where they are embraced by their Savior.

Another scene depicts two college girls at a party where a man offers them drugs—"My salvation comes in little white packages," he says—and they both shoot up and overdose amidst a flurry of horrifying noises, vocal distortions, and lighting effects. When they come to their senses, they realize they have died. In their despair they try to console one another. But when they ask the angel if their names are in the Book of Life, the angel sadly turns away and the devil comes out, taunting them with the line about "salvation in little white packages," and drags them violently off stage.

There are a number of other powerful scenes in the drama, including people who are reunited with their children in heaven and other families that are torn apart because only some of them believed.

After I confirmed that we would host the drama, I kept on sowing the seeds of revival and building up a vision in the people's hearts to see great things happen as a result of our outreaches to the community. I wanted that Great Commission church, the beacon in a time of darkness, and I knew it would take a believing people to see it happen. "If you are not being stirred, then I am not doing my job," I told the congregation one Sunday. "These sermons are meant to build up a revivalist spirit in your hearts."

In early January of 1994, I told the people that God had laid it on my heart to spend the first month of my pastorate preaching on revival. I told them the church was going to fill up with new converts, but first we had to have revival in our individual lives and in our church's prayer and worship. Many of us had head knowledge of the Scriptures, but not experience—in other words, we heard the Word of the Lord and still we walked out of the service wondering if it would be convenient to apply it to our lives that week.

I told them then, and I reiterate now, that as Christians, we do not have a choice in obedience, period. Either we are living it, or we are being disobedient; either we are claiming the promises of God, or we do not believe in them.

I preached a message titled "The Few, the Strong, the Remnant": I told the church that God always has a remnant of people desirous to know Him more, to see great things done in His name, willing to do whatever it takes for the cause of Christ. The remnant will see revival, for no revival has ever occurred without them. In the beginning, the disciples were the remnant; but even among the disciples, Peter, James, and John were closer to Jesus than the others. They were a special remnant unto the Lord. Of all the people He fed and healed and touched and preached to, just a few were willing to go the distance.

There is always a remnant somewhere, and there are always those in the church who have such a presence of God in their lives that they cannot stand compromise with the world. They do not indulge in questionable movies, music, or television shows, dirty jokes, or criticism of God and the church, corrupting their godly nature. Instead, they are zealous to win souls, eager to shine their light in a depraved world. As a result of the work of the remnant, I told the congregation, hundreds—even thousands—could be saved, because miracles follow remnant people. The remnant are the foundation for a move of God; they become the hammer in the hand of omnipotence.

God used remnant people in every great work in the Bible. Remnant people wrote the Old and New Testaments, led Israel into the desert, and led God's people into battle. But the remnant is always misunderstood and often persecuted. Remember Noah's family? The disciples? The Early Church? Lot? Moses? Think of all those who were willing to do anything in the service of God, and you will have a long list of people the world distrusted and despised. Then I posed the question to the church: Were we remnant people? Were we willing to be that hammer in the hand of God? The purpose of the remnant message was to set the standard for our church, the standard of the remnant, God's chosen people. But I took it a step further, and from that point on I began to treat the church as a remnant, because if a person or a people knows that you expect certain things of them, they will eventually begin to behave that way.

As it turned out, there was a remnant already in Modesto, made up of pastors who met on Wednesday mornings to pray together for the city. These men of God wanted to break down denominational barriers and become unified as the body of Christ to reach their neighborhoods, and in doing so I believe they brought God's favor to Modesto.

I wanted the people in my church to get in on the prayer action, to have sore knees. I wanted the carpets at the altar to be bare in testimony to the many hours they spent praying for the lost. I told them that Satan loves the preacher who skips up to the pulpit with the good news that their church just won top honors in the bowling league, but he fears the preacher that prays with eternity blazing in his eyes. Satan loves the believer's kick-back-and-be-raptured attitude, but he trembles when we strategize and attack. Revival brings fear to hell because the Church swaps fashion for passion, amusement for amazement, and superficial faith for supernatural faith.

I laid out several things that happen when revival occurs. First, our words and our life become inseparable and we are finally acting how we believe. If we say we are Christians, and then we go out and tell dirty jokes or do poor work on the job, we are actively leading people away from God. We are, in fact, antiwitnesses, Pharisees, and hypocrites. And I reminded them that Jesus reserved his harshest words for religious hypocrites.

Second, when revival hits, the importance of inner character becomes paramount: righteousness, honesty, integrity, faithfulness, obedience—all become your goals. Outside indicators like job and wealth and status seem less important, because root changes take place in one's life.

Third, when revival occurs you take revenge on sin. Proverbs 8:13 says "The fear of the Lord is to hate evil." Is it okay to hate? Sure, if it's evil, pride, arrogance, the perverse mouth, filthy things, and the like. When people are redeemed from sin, they want to turn around and attack that sin. Take a moment and think about the people in the specific ministries in your church: prison ministry, ministry to prostitutes, homosexuals, drug users, adulterers. Isn't it true that many of the people involved in those ministries were people who once led those lifestyles and now have a burden to turn it around and use it to glorify Christ? I call it taking a stick and beating the devil, because the thing the devil hates probably more than anything is when one person escapes his trap and goes back to rescue ten more. It deprives him of trophies in his Museum of Fools.

The fourth thing that happens when revival hits is that people move out of the comfort zone and become witnesses. There are no more pew potatoes, because people begin to live their Christianity, not just profess it as a creed. The church sanctuary is no longer a nursery for the comfort-seeking Christian, but a staging ground for believers to go out and fight.

In February I introduced my vision for the church, first preaching on Habakkuk 1:5. "'Look at the nations and watch—Be utterly astounded! For I will work a work in your days which you would not believe, though it were told you.'" I titled the vision "Fruitfulness and Increase" and professed my belief that the coming year would bring the greatest harvest the church had ever seen.

Just after that we, as a church, began a forty-day fast to bring the vision to pass in Modesto. Each one of us signed up for a day or a series of days to fast, and we arranged the names on a big display board so that at least one person was fasting on each of the forty days. In reality there were hundreds fasting on each of those days because the people were believing that their city would be won.

I told them we would see a day when we would have two Sunday morning services, filling the balcony each time. I told them we would have to build new facilities on our twenty-five-acre property to contain the influx of people from the city. But I also made it clear that we were not going to fill up the church by becoming seeker-sensitive. In other words, we were not going to make Sunday nights "casual night" with a short little service so that everyone could go out and eat ice cream afterwards. If they wanted that kind of church, I suggested they go elsewhere, because I had never been a man pleaser; I had always been a God pleaser. We were not going to shorten the message just to keep people from experiencing conviction. Ice cream socials didn't convict the soul. Coming into contact with Christ did, and that was the goal of our church—heavenly contact, not human comfort. We

113

were going to reach the community on our terms, not the community's terms, because the community's terms had failed long ago. We were going to offer the lost something new, something they needed. We were going to get our noses out of the history books, quit talking about the revivals of old, and start doing what we knew would bring revival in our day, before our very eyes.

"Some of you in the church say, 'Why Modesto?'" I said one Sunday morning. "I say, 'Why not Modesto?' I'm not in this city to play games. I'm here to do battle! Some of you say 'We had revival fifty years ago.' I say, 'We can have revival now!'"

I have always loved visual demonstrations and illustrated sermons because they grab people's attention more than words alone. One Sunday evening I had a basketball hoop up on the stage with me to demonstrate what a Notre Dame basketball coach had done years ago with his team. He was going into a game against a team that had won eighty-eight games in a row—a sure defeat for his own team. But for a whole week the coach made his team cut down the net after each practice, like a winning team does after a game. He wanted them to visualize victory. At first they thought it was silly, but by the end of the week they had done it so much that they believed in their ability to win. They could visualize it. Indeed, they did win against that unbeaten team, and when they did, they cut down the net, just as they had visualized for a week during practice.

On that Sunday night I brought up each member of our staff and had them name their vision and cut the net for victory. Our Bible college administrator cut the net for three hundred students to enroll. Our youth pastor cut the net for five hundred saved in the upcoming year. Our children's pastor cut the net for five hundred children in his services. I cut the net for massive revival in the city of Modesto and for our church to be crowded to the walls with the lost being found.

For a solid year I preached revival in Modesto, revival in the Central Valley, revival in our homes, revival in our church. I preached it as hard as I could, and I repeated it over and over and over, challenging, prodding, poking, putting up the vision, dreaming the dream out loud, so we would have something to focus on. I made no apologies for seizing the promises of God, for they were ours already. I used all the evangelistic fire I could generate on that platform, but, of course, whatever fire I had was not enough. It took a believing people and a willing God. I told them that the time was coming to put it on the line, to stop talking and to step out in faith, to take the risk, to act like remnant people, to run toward the city—not away from it like Jonah did, to take the promise of revival in hand and deliver it to the city. The time was coming, I said. The Spirit would direct us, and we would have to lay it on the line.

"Get ready," I said to the people of God. "Get ready."

Chapter 23

Fifteen Thousand Tickets

A s a pastor it is easy to tell when the dream begins to take on reality and the people are behind you, when they see the vision you see, when they are pressing toward the same goal. It's almost like being the coach of a team when the tide of enthusiasm turns, when the crowd begins to cheer in your favor, and you feel the surge behind you. The active church has an energy about it, a spirit of excitement that you can sense as you drive into the parking lot. It's not a cold place, it is hot with electricity. People are not acting like God's frozen people, they are acting like God's chosen people.

In the early winter of 1994 we moved into the Christmas season and put on a big musical, "Angel Tree," which looked exactly like the name says. After the holiday season everyone sighed with relief after expending so much money and energy in the month of December. But

I couldn't rest, knowing that our drama presentation was only two weeks away. I had to immediately begin planning and promoting it.

Getting people excited about anything in early January is nearly impossible. The big productions have been done, the kids are going back to school, the parents are getting their feet on the ground again, and everyone is preoccupied thinking about the new year. The least likely item among their New Year's resolutions is going to a drama about heaven and hell, especially after having just seen one about the birth of Christ.

But I knew that "Heaven's Gates & Hell's Flames" was going to be powerful. So with only two weeks to publicize it and get our people to support it, I ordered fifteen thousand tickets, and as a church we committed ourselves to distributing them to the unsaved. I bundled the tickets in groups of five because a single one was too easy to mislay or discard, regardless of the resolve of the distributor. As the tickets disappeared from the table in the foyer, I could only hope that they were all making it into the hands of nonbelievers.

As a demonstration of belief to the church, I participated fully in the ticket distribution. Debbie and I passed them out everyplace we went: restaurants, grocery stores, drug stores, barbers, banks. We used every encounter with the lost as an opportunity to give away tickets. We also had posters made up and got every businessperson in the church to display them at their work. Even then, it was hard to know how many people were taking us seriously. Here we had free tickets to a drama no one had ever heard of before, and with a name like "Heaven's Gates & Hell's Flames," it probably looked like we were going to give them one full hour of fire and brimstone preaching—a modern-day version of "Sinners in the Hands of an Angry God." At the same time, people in the community seemed to appreciate getting the tickets, but we never knew if they held onto them, if they lost them in a purse or glove compartment, or if they were just being polite and waiting until we were out of our sight to throw them away.

Nevertheless, by the time the drama rolled around, all fifteen thou-

117

sand tickets had been distributed throughout the Modesto community.

I also had to convince our church that the drama would be a success so they would feel good about bringing unsaved family and friends. Unfortunately, I didn't have many ways to show them how powerful it would be, no video footage, no photographs or newspaper articles. But I did have reports from other churches that had sponsored the drama and had experienced great results. One church about our size in Dallas had recently seen two thousand people saved in two weeks with "Heaven's Gates." There were rumors that a church in Baton Rouge had seen close to eighteen thousand people saved—which was too high a number for us to even imagine. It was beyond what we felt we could expect, so I stuck to the Dallas example.

"Two thousand people were saved in Dallas at this drama," I said on Sunday mornings. "We need to pray for two thousand saved here in Modesto."

Even then I felt like two thousand was the limit of what we could reasonably expect. One thousand was closer, I felt, to what could happen if things went well, and even that was inspiring.

Then I had the church get actively involved in outreach. There was a particular demonstration I had done as a youth pastor that drew a lot of attention, in the end, leading to a lot of salvations. In our youth meeting I had given everyone a card and asked them to write down the name of a friend they had in the city who they wanted to see saved before the end of the school year. The next week I had the cards—hundreds of them—posted on a display board, and as these friends were saved, I moved the card with their name on it to the other side of the display, indicating their salvation. If no one had responded I could have looked like the biggest fool in youth ministry; the board could have sat there for a year and gotten dusty, with no salvations, no movement of the cards. It was risky business.

For the first month or so of this demonstration, only seven people came forward whose names had been on the cards, but I was determined that it not become a hollow exercise. I needed to jolt the saved youth into realizing the gravity of their friends' situations, so I took it one step further. I made duplicates of several of the cards, and at our next youth meeting I spoke on the reality of hell. In the middle of the message I took those names down and read them off, "Billy . . . Sally . . . Annie . . . Steve . . ." As I did, I placed them in a bowl, poured lighter fluid on them, and set them on fire.

"Hell is real, people," I said while the flames danced before their stunned eyes, "and these people are going there."

Our youth group was jolted into action, and our attendance boomed. We had stacks and stacks of cards on the altar every week, and those people were getting saved, all because we stepped out in faith, because we cared about those people, and we wanted them to join our family, the family of God.

I adapted the presentation for Modesto and an adult audience: no flames, no lighter fluid. I knew the people would respond without extreme measures. First I had everyone in the congregation write down names of every unsaved person they knew in Modesto. Some people had only two or three names, but others had lists a yard long. Then we spread the lists on the altar, and during a three-day fast a week before the drama, we prayed over them, walking up and down the aisles, picking up the pieces of paper and reading off the names to personalize our prayers. During the noon hour people sacrificed their lunches to come from work and pray with us; the whole church's energy was focused on the lost.

The drama team of David and Laurie Ford from Reality Outreach arrived with little publicity on Friday, January 13, to start setting up the production. I had already announced the need for volunteer actors and stagehands the previous Sunday, and we had put an announcement in our bulletin for about fifty to seventy-five people to be involved in the drama. I talked to staff and choir members and other people I thought might be interested and asked them to show up that Friday for first rehearsals. They didn't know exactly what they were volunteering for, other than that it was a drama about heaven and hell, and we hadn't taken names or done anything official, so we didn't know who would show up until Friday evening. They were all from our congregation; not a professional among them—no actors, no stage technicians, no lighting experts, no trained sound men, no acting coaches, no production managers. It was just a bunch of amateurs doing their best with what they had to expand God's kingdom of light.

The first thing they did was to construct a huge stage on our church platform, which was pretty large to begin with. They didn't even finish constructing the set that night—which consisted of a stairway to heaven and multileveled platforms for the angels to stand on—let alone start reading the parts. That didn't begin until Saturday. But what the Fords were doing while everyone helped construct the set was observe people, looking for the servants, getting to know them, and making mental notes of who would fit best into which roles. Then, on Saturday afternoon, they finally pulled out the script and began testing out parts, which was an adventure all its own. Some people would read the part of the devil, and it would sound humorous or gentle—not the way a devil is supposed to sound at all. Others would roam around the stage looking like the hunchback of Notre Dame. Everyone had an individual style, but it was amazing to see the unlikeliest people come to life as they acted out a particular part. Something would pull the unseen talent out of them, another side of them would appear, and they would fill a role perfectly.

The first performance was scheduled for Sunday night, so I hung around the periphery watching the practice, hoping my people would have their lines memorized in time, wondering how they were going to put it all together by the following afternoon. I knew it would happen and that people would come and lives would be changed, but I was not at all prepared for the response to our first performance.

Chapter **24**

A Military Tactic

"Christians" were popping up all around Doug, and try as he might, he couldn't avoid them anymore. From the day he'd walked out of Cagney's bar as a sign of protest, he had vowed not to be suckered into submission by Lane's gentle entreaties. Behind every kind request, Doug knew, lay a concealed motive, a land mine, a trap. There were just as many traps in religion as in prison or in war, at least that had been his experience.

In the summer of 1994 Doug had momentarily given in to Lane's efforts to brainwash him. He had gone to church and tried to make a change in his own life, hoping it could be salvaged from the wreckage of prison, war, and hatred. For a few months he had tried to live the life that others said he ought to live.

But soon after he had made his pact with God to do better, his fiancée—the woman he wanted to pledge his life to—had broken up with him. Slapped in the face by her rejection, Doug thought he had learned a lesson about God: As soon as you gave into Him, He took everything away and beat you, maybe not in the physical sense, but in the emotional sense, just like Doug's foster parents had so many years ago.

Doug went back to the life he knew: the drinking, the fights, the biker attitude. He didn't care how many of his friends turned chicken, Doug Adams would never abandon the ethic of the outlaw: Trust no one and to thine own self be true. Doug's true self had been shaped in foster homes and on the road with his biker gang, in the jungles of Vietnam and in Klan meetings. His true self had been proven over and over for forty-six years, and now he wore it like a badge of honor. He would never give it up.

"I like the music and the people," said Squeaky, formerly one of Doug's closer buddies. "They don't make you feel like dirt. They make you feel like you belong there."

Doug's defenses went up as he stared into the glossy coat of varnish on the bar counter. Suddenly, he didn't like Squeaky so much. But in his heart of hearts he was beginning to have second thoughts about his antichurch strategy. If he really wanted to shut them up, maybe he ought to just go again and then be done with it. They wouldn't have anything more to bug him about. It was like retreating to the hills in order to take the valley. It wasn't really retreat; it was a military tactic. If it worked, it would save him a month of grief, having to ward off request after request. He could ease back into the lifestyle he was comfortable with. Maybe then the whole subject would just go away.

He decided to do it, no matter how bad it was.

"Hey, Lane, I'll go again," he said.

All the patrons turned to look at him.

"What?" Lane said.

"I'll do it. I'll go see your sissy preacher, and then I'll come back here and I'll be the same person I ever was. Things never change for Doug Adams."

Doug's buddies stared at each other with a knowing look.

"Okay, Doug, how about tomorrow night? They're starting a play, and I've been handing out tickets. Should be pretty good," Lane said.

"Tomorrow is as good as any," Doug said between sips of his whiskey. "In fact, I'm eager to get it over with. Sooner the better."

"Great," said Lane with a smile as wide as the bar itself. "I'll drive."

Chapter 25

Witnessing a Miracle

When I pulled into the church parking lot that rainy Sunday evening, I was astounded at how many people had come to the drama, especially considering all the unfavorable conditions. Our orange-suited parking lot crew was swamped by the stream of cars feeding into our lot. Nearby shopping centers filled up, and people walked a half mile in the rain because they were so eager to get there, drawn by the power of the Spirit.

That first night's presentation was one of the most incredible and anointed events I have ever witnessed, not because of the acting, but because of the palpable presence of God that had drawn the crowd there and was working in their hearts. The drama was powerfully anointed; the actors' lines were like wine of the Spirit to the audience; people were drinking it all in, their facial expressions reflecting the drama before them; and you could feel the bondages of sin breaking in that crowded sanctuary. When the last lines were spoken and the triumphant music played, the audience erupted into applause because their hearts had been touched in a way they had never felt before. David Ford and I went onstage, and he gave an invitation to receive Christ Jesus—the One who had touched their hearts that night and the only One who could guarantee their passage into heaven. As soon as he said those words, over eight hundred people got up from their seats and walked down the aisle.

Imagine it for a moment: eight hundred people standing to their feet and then coming toward to you in a wave of deliverance, each one of them wanting to make a commitment to Jesus. It was almost like watching the Israelites walking through the Red Sea. I was witnessing a miracle. For a moment my staff and I did not know what to do with them all because we had never seen so many people respond at one time. The altar was full of bruised and battered souls who needed our attention. What we normally did was take them into another room, give them some reading material, pray with them, and give them some time to themselves to draw close to their Savior. That night we had prepared the prayer chapel for three hundred to four hundred people—not nearly enough room for all of the converts.

We had prepared a total of five hundred salvation packets for all three nights for those who responded to the altar call. In each packet was a card for them to fill out, a ballpoint pen, and some information about Christ, their commitment, and our church. Within minutes the packets were gone, and we needed hundreds more. Whatever preparations we had made—in our limited understanding of what might take place—were quickly overwhelmed by what the Lord was doing among us. As a church we felt like the child trying to keep up with his father who has him by the hand but is running so fast that the child's feet touch the ground only every few yards.

We ended up taking the extra people into the classrooms in our adjacent school building, filling the rooms up one after another. When we ran out of salvation packets, we grabbed index cards and whatever else we could get our hands on and had them write their names and phone numbers down so we could contact them later.

I was amazed to see people get saved who had never been to church before, like the one young man who came up to me and gave me a handkerchief representing his gang colors—inside was a knife.

"Here," he said, "I want you to have this. I don't need it anymore."

My eyes were opened to the magnitude of what was happening in our city. These were not just church people rededicating their lives, though many did—these were sinners straight from the streets, people who had lived hard lives and had driven away their loved ones, people who had done bad things and never felt the cleansing effect of forgiveness. In one wave of His magnificent hand, God was bringing them home to an eternal family.

Chapter 26

Too Many Getting Saved

O vernight, lightning from heaven had struck our church and electrified the entire city of Modesto, leaving us reeling and rejoicing at the same time. The second and third nights of the drama were even more powerful than the first, with more people coming forward to receive Christ. There was as many as a thousand each night standing shoulder to shoulder on the platform waiting to be led in prayer so that they could know the Lord. Word of the awakening ran like a current through the community; the city itself was beginning to stir with excitement and expectation, in the workplace, in the schools, in the bars, and over the backyard fences. After the third night, which was supposed to be our last performance, I made the decision to keep the drama going so that more people could see it and be saved.

No sooner had we decided to keep the drama going than we ran into a logistical nightmare—the kind of nightmare every church dreams of having. We simply had too many people coming to the drama every night and getting saved! As a church we had never been in such a position before, where we had to accommodate a huge influx of people every night in a safe and logical manner using all volunteer work. The drama had gone from being a three-night ministry to a continuous production that reaped incredible results with each performance. As the response continued, the monumental task of putting everything in place every day before each performance fell to a group of people who had never been trained in crowd control or security or stage productions or even how to deal with huge numbers of people wanting to give their lives to the Lord. We were a church, not a professional tent crusade.

I called an emergency meeting of our staff to discuss all the ramifications of what was happening. The first thing we decided was that our old system of leading the new converts into the prayer chapel after the service was inadequate—we would have needed four prayer chapels to hold them all. The number of people getting saved every night was greater than the congregation of a large church! Instead, we decided to bring them to the altar area—which included the entire stage, stairway to heaven, angel platforms, everything—and pray with them there. We were giving every new believer a salvation packet and had been accustomed to handing them out personally, but now they needed to be distributed en masse. And instead of retrieving them by hand we bought a number of huge plastic tubs and had the new believers put their filled-out material in them. We felt rather like the disciples gathering up the surplus bread and fish and finding that our baskets could hardly contain it all.

Our supply of prayer packets had been exhausted on the first night, so we had to form a volunteer assembly line to copy, sort, and collate two thousand packets for each night. The copy machines in the church office never stopped running—and neither did the staff. The phones were ringing, the machines were humming, the toner in the copier was constantly running out; both office resources and personnel were being pushed to the limit. We had to overnight more office supplies because regional stores had run out of what we needed. I felt like God had dropped a bomb on our city—a good bomb—and our whole church was scrambling to meet the need.

God was shaking our city.

Thank God for a church full of servants! Men and women by the hundreds volunteered to be ushers, parking lot attendants, security assistants, nursery volunteers, altar counselors, food preparation assistants, follow-up callers, photocopiers, staplers, folders, ticket takers, cleanup crew members, and whatever else we needed. The people knew that revival had hit, and everything else in their lives seemed to fade into the background: Work, social life, entertainment, and relaxation, all of those normal concerns no longer mattered. When Christ comes alive in your city, a clear line is drawn between things eternal and things transitory. The transitory things simply don't matter anymore, and even people who are in a bored or slothful state come back to life when God moves, jolted out of their slothfulness into action. We had volunteers coming in day and night to assist in every way they could, to put their hands to the plow. It was a season of harvest, and all hands were in the fields. As the drama went on for the remainder of that week, the momentum continued to build, and more and more people in our church were stirred deep within their souls to become a part of what was happening.

There were eight inches of water standing in many parts of our visitors' parking lot, but parking lot attendants came straight from work, skipping dinner, and worked in the pouring rain night after night, guiding cars in with lighted batons and the smiles on their faces. One of them even got hit by a car and still he kept on working, because the feeling for and dedication to what was happening was not confined to the sanctuary alone. It spilled over into the parking lot as well: The attendants were enthusiastic because they knew they were the first contact people would have with the church, the first step toward their getting saved or seeing a loved one get saved. Finding a parking space was a significant achievement for someone who wanted to attend. It meant that they could probably get inside that night, and once you were inside, the spirit of the drama and the presence of God were almost certain to turn you or a loved one to the Lord. There was a sense that something major was going on—something that produced results—and that if you or your husband or your wife or your kids could just get in, the rest would take care of itself.

To help our attendants maintain their bright outlooks we bought reflective orange vests and rain suits for them to wear so they wouldn't get hit by any more cars, and also to give them a certain authority. At first we hesitated to spend much of our capital resources for the things we needed to support the production, things like the reflective vests. Initially we had rented radios and barricades for the parking attendants and security to use; we simply did not know how long we would need them. As hopeful observers of what the Lord was doing, we had to plan on the revival continuing through the next week, but we didn't know that it would. But after a week and a half, we saw that daily rentals could end up costing as much as buying the equipment, so we invested in all the parking lot equipment, and in the end, that was a wise move.

Our goal was to touch people with friendliness and a welcome spirit from the moment they entered our parking lot to the moment they left. First there were the parking attendants who established the church's attitude with their smiles and cheerful manner, then there were the parking lot greeters who guided people on foot to the sanctuary. They didn't just point to where the visitors ought to go, they took them there, and along the way they mentioned everything a visitor would need to know, for example, the availability of nursery care. When people got to the front door they encountered our front door greeters, who shook their hands and welcomed them to the church. Then they were passed to the ushers, who really had the toughest jobs of all—they were in charge of seating everybody. Not only that, but ushers had to deal with the crowd for two hours before each performance, keeping them out of the aisles, settling disputes about seat saving, and generally acting as the church's authority figures. People took their seating very seriously, and it was the ushers' job to finally decide when a seat could no longer be saved and had to be given up to accommodate someone else. Countless times the ushers heard, "They're just in the bathroom, give me five more minutes." The looks of desperation in some of those people's eyes made the ushers' job difficult and even though they felt great compassion for the people, the ushers stuck to their job like champions.

I had put together teams to do visitation and follow-up, but they were quickly dwarfed by the task of driving to every house and speaking with every person who had come forward. So instead of actually visiting them, we began to call them by phone, from nine in the morning to nine at night, fifteen hundred or more calls were made a day, beginning on the day after our first performance. Even that task was monstrous, but those volunteers stepped up to the plate and hit a home run every time, because they succeeded in getting back to all the new converts within a day of their decision. We felt it was crucial that they hear from us immediately and that they be encouraged to attend church that following Sunday in order to solidify their commitment.

This was the "retain" part of a win-and-retain ministry that had become such a vital part of my evangelistic credo, and it served us well. I didn't want just to have an impressive number of souls saved that I could tell my preacher friends about; I wanted to celebrate with those people on the Day of Judgment because their commitment had been lasting.

Our goal was not to have the biggest church in town, nor was it to get every single convert to come to Calvary Temple. We just wanted to get them in touch with Christ. After that, they could choose whichever church they wanted, so long as it was Christ-centered and doctrinally sound. When we made the phone calls, we never told them to come to our church; rather, we asked if they already attended church. If they didn't, we encouraged them to get plugged into a congregation in the area so their new life could be nurtured.

To help those new believers who chose to attend Calvary Temple we immediately started a New Life class, which met on Sunday mornings. It was intended to address the practicalities of the faith, the most common questions they would ask themselves, the issues they would face in their day-to-day lives. For example, how do I speak to God? When are my prayers most effective? Are the prayers of ministers more effective than mine? How do I know when I am hearing from God? How does Jesus Christ fit into my life? What is the role of the Holy Spirit? We understood that a person's initial contact did not establish a life pattern, did not lay a foundation for faith, and did not draw the believer into a daily walk with God. It merely stirred the soul and invited a commitment to Christ that needed to be encouraged and instructed by the church and by the believer's own prayer and contact with the Bible. That was the purpose of the New Life class, to be there when the excitement wore off and the growing began.

Within just a few days of the first night, the news had gotten around town that incredible things were happening at Calvary Temple, and people began coming earlier and earlier. The drama began at seven o'clock, but people started coming at six o'clock, then five, then four, then three o'clock in the afternoon, to stand in the wind and rain to wait for a seat. Thousands of people formed lines that snaked out across our property, and when we opened the doors, they ran across the foyer and into the sanctuary as if it were hosting some sort of rock concert—people were storming our church to hear about heaven and hell. For the first time in my experience, people were crowding the doors to get the good news about salvation.

As I continued to invite people, they didn't believe me when I began telling them they should come two hours early for seats. They moseyed in a half hour early and were turned away, an hour early— turned away, two hours early—turned away. The demand for seats was so great that people would go to great lengths to get them and hold onto them; just like the parking spaces, those seats represented souls saved. But with the onslaught of early arrivers came a new problem: The cast and crew were losing out on parking spaces; so the drama could go on, we had to designate parking for them and then assume the unpleasant task of guarding it. Then we noticed that half of the parking crew was disappearing at about seven o'clock, just when the drama was starting. They were going out for fast food for everyone because most of them had come straight from work without eating. So we took the cue and began providing a group dinner, which fostered a greater spirit of unity among the various groups of people whose tasks were making the drama possible.

If we had eliminated any one group—nursery attendants, ushers, parking attendants, security, actors(!), altar workers—the whole thing would have fallen apart. The crew and volunteers had become like a giant organism that would be crippled by a missing part. The congregation had their own spirit of participation: They were putting the visitors' welfare above their own, welcoming the whole community. What a glorious sight it was to see such servanthood in action right before my very eyes! The true mettle of a church is seen in the demanding times, when the call to action is immediate and believers must respond like warriors summoned into battle.

Every night as it went on and on, I stood on the platform, watching a sea of people swirl around the stage, and wondered, *God, is this going to continue?* It was completely out of my control. I had no idea if it would drop off suddenly, taper off over a few nights, or keep going as strongly as it had for the first few days. I asked Rudy Krulik what normally happened (keeping in mind that this was anything but a normal event), and he said attendance most often wound down of its own accord and that we should be able to tell when it had peaked.

People continued lining the walls and jamming the aisles (though we tried to keep that from happening too much so that the fire marshall wouldn't shut us down); they sat on the decorative ledges and crowded the foyer just to get a glimpse of the stage.

But they were not there to see a spectacle, they were there because they wanted a change in their lives. There was an eagerness and excitement about coming in contact with Jesus among the three thousand people who attended each night. At times the clapping and shouting was frequent and prolonged; the audience participated fully in the drama's high and low points, actually yelling at the devil and encouraging characters to make the right decision.

Many people would weep in their seats, because one's attention was on the status of one's own soul, one's eternal destiny. It was a time of introspection and surrender, of repentance and salvation, a roll call for the redeemed to see who was coming to the great banquet in the sky. I saw tough men crying as they stood at the altar following me in prayer. My wife, Debbie, stood next to me and wept every night over the sheer beauty of seeing so many people come to the Lord. If you have ever felt the touch of God on your soul, if you have ever felt so near to Him that nothing else matters, if you have ever seen the tears streaming down the faces of children and their parents as they are embraced in the arms of a loving God, you know what we were experiencing.

Already, thousands of testimonies were pouring into our office, and as we read them, we thanked and praised God for the glory and grace He was showing in our city.

Coming Home

I t had been over a decade and a half since Tammy Jones had attended church outside of the county jail when a friend of hers called in January of 1995 and invited her to a drama at Calvary Temple. Her friend was not a Christian, but she had heard about the drama from a workmate. Because Tammy had nothing better to do, she said she would go along and bring Earl, now in junior high.

When they got to the church, Tammy got out of the car and looked across the grassy area toward the main building, amazed at how many people were packing into the sanctuary. Inside, she had never seen so many people in one building, and as more came they began to line the walls and the aisles. Fortunately, her habit was to arrive early, and her group didn't have to struggle for a seat.

Being in church put Tammy in a reflective frame of mind, though she had not come for a spiritual experience; she had come to be entertained. As she sat in the pew and waited for the show to begin, she thought back on all the things she'd gone through. It had been twenty-six years since the first time her mother had abandoned her, twenty-three years since she had been taken advantage of sexually by countless transient drunks, twenty years since she was forced to have an abortion, and nine years since two of her children had died. She had been clean of drugs for four years and had finally found a man that treated her with respect. But through all of those good things, there was something still missing from her life. She felt no purpose, no peace, no rhyme or reason for her tortured life. She was still searching for the missing piece of the puzzle.

As the drama started that evening, Tammy's heart began to soften, despite herself. The actors said their lines, the music played, and people were welcomed into heaven or hell. As the play went on, the Holy Spirit pried open her spirit and began to pour himself in. She saw her own life in the scenes on stage, especially when a family was reunited in heaven with children who had died.

When the offer was given to come forward and accept Jesus, both Tammy and Earl went forward to make a permanent change in their lives. For twenty years Tammy had not cried—the drugs had numbed her emotions—but the tears streamed down as the Lord poured in forgiveness.

As new believers gathered for prayer, ministers from the church laid hands on them, and Tammy experienced an incredible feeling of peacefulness and resolution. For the first time she wasn't wondering what she was doing or why she was alive or what her purpose was. Remembering the past didn't hurt, and as for all the things she had done in her life to hurt herself and others—she knew they were gone, forgotten forever, because of the blood of Jesus. That was a promise she knew she would hold onto the rest of her life.

God had never abandoned the little girl from Martinez, even as His heart broke at the circumstances she faced. He had her marked for salvation from day one. Finally, after a lifetime of searching, Tammy had come home.

Chapter 28

"From Dopehead to Hope-Head"

*I*n the winter of his freshman year, Javier began hearing about a play being put on by a local church. All his friends, even his teachers, were talking about it. Javier was curious about what exactly was going on, but he had no way of finding out. Then one night his aunt came home and announced that she was taking him to the play. (In her own mind, she was searching for something to counteract the bad influences in his life.) Though she had raised the children Catholic and never considered attending other churches, even for special events, something whispered to her spirit that this might be the thing Javier needed to turn himself around.

Javier went to the drama with his aunt, defiant but curious. He didn't think he was ready to give up the things in life that brought him happiness: his gang friends, the drugs, the alcohol, the girlfriends. But the drama moved him deeply, giving him a framework of truth he had never known before. By the end of the presentation he was ready to accept Jesus Christ as his personal Savior. His young heart was affected in a way that chemicals and rebellion never could affect it. He was particularly touched by the scene where two young women took drugs at a party, overdosed, and were dragged to hell. Javier, the rebel and druggie, was riveted by the depiction and felt like he was watching himself on the stage. He saw how the devil was deceiving the party-girls with promises of better and better highs, and he realized how the devil was deceiving him too. He realized that drugs were not the answer he was looking for—Jesus was.

When all the members of the congregation were invited to accept Christ, Javier's hand shot up. He eagerly went forward to the altar and suddenly felt liberated and cleansed from his bitterness and anger—like a heavy backpack had been lifted off his shoulders.

"You should have seen that guy!" his aunt told her friends later. "He was crying and crying when he went to the altar. He hugged me and said he was feeling something inside. He came back with a different attitude."

Javier's life habits changed immediately. He began attending Calvary Temple every Sunday and most days in between. He stopped drinking, smoking, and taking drugs. He stopped experimenting sexually. He even stopped swearing. His grades that semester jumped to C's with a few A's sprinkled in. More importantly, his inner character had been changed. He glowed with excitement and smiled broadly when talking about the Lord. He was learning to be kind rather than coldhearted, forgiving rather than vindictive, loving rather than angry.

"I went from a drug dealer to a Bible reader, and from a dopehead to a hope-head," he said. "I have been witnessing to my friends, and I tell them why Jesus died for us. I know that God wants to do something in my life. Praise the Lord, man! I love Jesus!"

Chapter 29

"I'm Not the Old Frank"

rank Tanner's problems were hardly over, though in his heart he knew that getting caught for his involvement in a counterfeiting scheme was the best thing that could have happened. Jail time was likely, so he sat at home and waited for the federal authorities to make the next move.

He felt horrible for what he had done, like a failed father and a failed human being. He needed direction and guidance; in desperation he turned to his next-door neighbor, who happened to be a member of Calvary Temple. Frank confessed his feelings and fears, and the neighbor invited him to church on Sunday. Almost overwhelmed by guilt, Frank went to church and then to the drama, and there he and his daughter gave their lives to the Lord.

The turnaround in his life was immediate. Before, his conversation was always riddled with profanities and vulgarities. Now he didn't speak that way at all. He gave up drinking, and his old friends were stunned. Even his mother could not believe it. "Is this the same guy?" she asked of him one day.

Frank and his daughter began attending church and special Bible classes, finding a peaceful way of living that they had never had before. Though his case was still pending before a federal court, Frank knew that when he started over next time, the Lord would be the center post of his life.

"Giving my life to the Lord was the greatest feeling I have ever had," he said. "I'm not the old Frank, that's for sure."

Indeed, he was nothing like the old Frank Tanner, angry at the world for his failures; he was content, living clean, and free, a new creation in Christ Jesus.

Chapter **30**

Welcomed Back

*D*oug Adams walked into the sanctuary of Calvary Temple with fear in his heart, fear that this would be his last stand, his last point of decision between an old, worn-out lifestyle and something brand new. He was afraid to break down in front of his friends and afraid to let down the walls that had protected him from inner harm for decades. But something had been tugging at him, and the tug had become too strong to ignore.

It happened to be the first night of the drama, as the rain poured down and the people crowded in. As Doug hung around he began to see something happen before his very eyes; people from the community that never would have set foot in a church were walking in. The Spirit began to move in Doug's heart—before the production even started. The crucial decision had been made, not by walking to the altar for recommitment, but in the quiet stillness of his soul. Doug had given in. There wasn't flash or fanfare. There was simply salvation.

Doug helped that night with the ushering. He had done some of that the summer before when he had tried church. Imagine the surprise of someone walking into a church and seeing an usher—complete in his usher coat—leading people to their pews with a knife hanging off his belt, a ten-gallon cowboy hat, and dark sunglasses.

The staff welcomed Doug back with open arms. He received what he needed: love in a way he had never known it. By receiving what Christians offered, he came into the Kingdom for good and became a brother in the Lord. At the age of forty-six, Doug Adams had found God, not at a bar or on a battlefield, but in church. God had kept him alive for that very day when Doug stopped being an enemy of righteousness and became a son of God.

Chapter 31

An Abundance of Testimonies

*E*very person who came forward those twenty-eight nights of the drama had a story to tell that would draw tears from even the most steely-eyed observer. We began to hand out small blue testimony forms for people to write down their testimonies, and we received thousands of them back. People recorded victories over struggles big and small, whether it was alcohol, a broken marriage, or chronic anger. The Lord touched people wherever they were at in their lives through the drama; no problem was too insignificant or too grand to be brought to light.

KIM, A YOUNG LADY FROM MODESTO, HAD HIT ROCK BOTTOM in her life and was close to suicide before she found hope at the drama that made her want to hold onto life. She was baptized in water at one of our Sunday night services, and she beamed and cried for joy as the rest of the congregation witnessed her decision for Christ.

MARTIE, FROM NEWMAN, WAS SAVED FROM LESBIANISM and witchcraft on January 30 at the drama. "I am no longer bound to chains of Satan. I've been set free!" she wrote.

A WOMAN AND HER HUSBAND WHO HAD STRUGGLED WITH ANGER and sexual alienation from one another were brought together in deeply personal ways that they had never experienced before. "My husband and I have a deeper intimacy now while we are serving Christ than we have had in the fourteen and a half years we've been married. We are talking, sharing, hugging, kissing, holding hands again. It's something I never dreamed possible," she wrote.

ANOTHER WOMAN WAS SAVED FROM HER ADDICTION TO GAMBLING, which had cost her and her husband tens of thousands of dollars.

PEGGY OF MODESTO WAS LIBERATED from her smoking habit.

JOHN OF MODESTO WROTE that "all the things and ideas I stood for before seem so ridiculous now that my eyes are open. Thank God for the change!"

CHUCK OF MODESTO GOT SAVED and wrote me a note that said, simply, "The devil better watch out now."

JOAN, ALSO OF MODESTO, was similarly brief: "I went. I saw. I believed. I've been saved."

DIANE OF ESCALON WAS SAVED with her two grandchildren, ages seven and eleven.

ROBERT, A HISPANIC MAN, said he had been "washed with Jesus, Clorox fresh"; after being baptized, even those "hard to remove sinful stains were gone."

CAROL BROUGHT SEVEN FAMILY MEMBERS, including her mother, father, aunt, cousin, and brother-in-law, and all were saved.

THE FRANCO FAMILY, WHO HAD BEEN REGULAR CATHOLICS, came to the drama on the first and second nights, and all six children—four teenage boys and two teenage girls—were saved and went out to buy Bibles with their own money. "This play has changed everything in our home," the mother wrote.

TONYA FROM RIVERBANK wrote that coming to the drama was life-changing, for she had been struggling with a lack of meaning and direction in her life. "I can't even begin to explain the changes," she said. "I know my name is in the Book of Life."

AARON BROUGHT SIX MEMBERS OF HIS FAMILY and all were saved. "I'm sure that my story can be told by many other families," he wrote. "I just thank God for the energy of all those who participated in the drama. I don't think we will ever feel or see the complete effect on the city that the drama has brought."

DON OF MODESTO AND HIS ESTRANGED SON from Galt, a city nearly an hour away, were reunited at our church altar after Don had been saved and was praying for his son's salvation. "All my prayers are now answered," Don said.

NASH FROM CERES WROTE that God directed him to the drama and "heard my cry for help. . . . There aren't enough words or enough paper to explain what God is doing in our lives to show His love, mercy, grace, and power."

RANDY BROUGHT HIS WIFE, TERESA, AND TWENTY OTHER PEOPLE to the drama, and they were saved. After finding Jesus, Teresa wrote to me, "My husband and I will donate our time to clean the hall or watch the nursery or give rides, etc. I know so many people to bring and so many ways to get them there. I called your office twice to tell you to keep the drama going."

JAMES OF MODESTO wrote, "My family is finally at peace!"

RUTH AND HER FOUR CHILDREN WERE SAVED and began attending church.

VIVIAN, A YOUNG LADY, WROTE, "I've been saved! I've given myself to the Lord; I read my Bible and attend church every Sunday. I go to the youth meetings on Wednesday, and I'm changed from the inside out."

ANGELA FROM SAN CARLOS WAS STRUGGLING with severe family problems when she attended. "I was desperate," she wrote. "My husband and I were about to get a divorce because we had so much anger. Now I pray every day for Jesus to show us the way. I have much more peace."

BOB AND DOLORES FROM OAKDALE wrote to me, "We went to your

church tonight and experienced 'Heaven's Gates & Hell's Flames.' Our lives have changed forever. Thank you for your commitment in doing God's work. Heaven's gates will see us someday, but hell's fire never will!"

ONE MAN WHO HAD PREVIOUSLY BEEN SAVED from a life of crime attended the drama one night. He had once stabbed another man, and it had weighed on his conscience for a long time. While he was praising God and watching people go forward to accept Christ, he saw the man he had stabbed going forward to give his life to Christ. Right there at the altar those two men had a meeting of reunion and forgiveness.

EVEN MY NEXT-DOOR NEIGHBORS had a tremendous turnaround. "My religious life had completely ended . . . until the Berteaus moved across the street. Glen and Debbie talked Sandy and me into seeing the drama. . . . For the first time in my life I was not being preached to about the Word of God, I was being spoken to. I don't know where my anger went or where this overwhelming feeling to give in to God and be saved came from, but it did. I got out of my seat, walked down to the altar, and said the words that put my name into the Book of Life," they wrote. Praise the Lord!

BUT THE AMAZING THING ABOUT THE REVIVAL was that it spilled over onto everyone, including the people in the church who had already received Christ. Many people who were in the drama itself had family that were not saved but came to the Lord as a result. Other people in the church were having experiences directly related to their desire to be servants and spread the word about the revival all over town.

ONE OF OUR USHERS BROUGHT IN EIGHTY-FIVE YOUTH from Sacramento, Lodi, Stockton, and Antioch, and sixty-two of them were saved. He was able to minister directly to their situations because he had recently kicked his own drug habit.

ANOTHER ONE OF OUR USHERS TOOK A WEEK OFF from work to give his time entirely to the church. "There was nothing like it," he said. "As we walked down to the front for the altar call each night, it was as if we walked through a curtain and into His presence. As I stood there facing the crowds, I was covered from the top of my head to my feet. His presence just radiated on and on and on, and it seemed that it would never lift. I felt the drawing power of it over and over again, and it was awesome."

A BUSINESSMAN IN OUR CHURCH invited his customers and fellow workers to the drama, and as a result, four employees were saved, and then the boss himself gave his heart to Jesus! The businessman continues to hear from his customers about the impact of the drama.

ONE WOMAN WHO CAME TO THE DRAMA had a job as a cashier at Wal-Mart, and when she returned to work she began telling customers about it as she checked out their items. Her conviction was so strong that many of them came and were also saved.

JILL, A WOMAN WHO HAD BEEN ATTENDING CALVARY for just over a year, had perhaps the most unique witnessing experience of all. She was in the middle of a medical condition that required her to be at the hospital on a regular basis. She found that the waiting rooms were filled with people talking about what was happening. "It became like a fellowship group, talking about God and things He had done in their lives," she told me. Given the schedule of doctors' offices it shouldn't surprise any of us that the "fellowship group" went on for three hours! Then, on another trip to Stanislaus Medical Center, Jill was able to witness to a doctor in the middle of a gynecological exam (in preparation for a hysterectomy) when the doctor herself initiated a conversation about the drama. Jill called it "odd and enlightening," and in my opinion it certainly proves that God will use us in every situation, anytime, anyplace.

THEN WE GOT WORD OF RUMBLINGS OVER AT THE HERSHEY'S chocolate plant in Oakdale, one of only two in the nation, where several of our church members worked. They had passed out tickets to fellow workers and then saw a revival in their company community—at least 102 people were saved, not counting people from the other two shifts.

A SCHOOL BUS DRIVER IN OUR CONGREGATION invited all of the youth on his bus to come to the drama, and over half of them got saved, including a gang member who then brought his "homies," who also got saved. They turned in their rags to the bus driver, who then wrote me a letter thanking us for bringing the drama to Modesto.

CHERYL OF MODESTO, A MIDDLE-AGED WOMAN WHO HARDLY EVEN WENT OUT AFTER DARK, was already a believer, but she was emboldened by the Holy Spirit to approach gang members in parking lots and malls to witness to them and invite them to the drama. An amazing thing happened when they showed up for the drama—the formerly rowdy young punks she had seen and feared on street corners and in empty parking lots were sitting in a church pew listening attentively to how they could be saved. The Lord had given Cheryl the ability to speak to these youth in such a way that they listened and responded. If He can do that, He can do anything!

FINALLY, MY LONG-STANDING WISH THAT I HAD HELD from the moment we came to Modesto came true when we began hearing from people at Gallo winery about changes in their priorities—from wine that you drink to wine that fills your life with song. One employee told us that testimonies and witnessing spread through the workplace and that supervisors, employees, and families were becoming Christians, creating a family within a family at the winery. Taking the winery for the Lord was a sweet conquest, like taking the command post of a region during battle. We were really cutting into the devil's territory!

As the first two weeks wore on, we received so many amazing testimonies that we had to start storing them in shipping boxes. Soon we hit our breaking point with the number of new life cards coming in; we simply could not keep up with them to invite them to church and extend a friendly, Christian hand. So we looked at the churches that were being represented at the altar, the ones that people knew were in their neighborhoods, or the churches that their friends went to, and counted about 250 of them from all over the Central Valley.

We decided to start sharing with these other churches the responsibility and privilege of following up new converts, so that their church could also grow from this move of God. I wrote a letter to each one, and we bundled up the cards and sent them off, a gesture that basically said, "God bless you; we love you; and we would love to see your church grow." Immediately the pastors came alive and responded by encouraging their people to go and take unsaved friends and family.

For years the pastors of churches from all denominations in Modesto had met once a week to pray for citywide revival, and now it was coming to pass. Those prayer meetings, many of which I had attended, laid the groundwork for cooperation between churches rather than competition. All too often churches get envious of one another, especially when good things are happening, and a barrier of pride blocks the work that can be done.

When a city is under enemy command, God does not want to bless just one church; He wants to bless the entire area. The churches in Modesto were a great example of interdenominational cooperation and love, and I am convinced that this contributed greatly to the work that was done in our city. As a result, the other congregations grew, and the revival that had begun as a spark in the Calvary Temple sanctuary was now catching fire all over the Central Valley.

Chapter 32

Traffic Jam at Coffee and Briggsmore

I stayed in consultation with Rudy Krulik and Dave Ford, because they had been presenting the drama for years. I was not of the mind that I would claim the ultimate right to control what was happening in my church. As it turned out, neither Dave nor Rudy had experienced anything like this production either. We were at the point where we had to call our own shots in faith; the maps had ended. You can guess how that felt—thrilling, frightening, startling, petrifying, and blessedly anointed, all at the same time.

I considered it significant that most of the people who were coming to see the drama were not repeat viewers. Every night I would ask people to raise their hands if it was their first time to see the drama. The average new attendance was between 85 and 95 percent, which meant that it was not just a church audience coming back repeatedly, it was people from the community: neighbors, coworkers, friends, colleagues, people who had read the newspaper reports or had seen the television coverage. This was verified every night after the performance: We found a colossal mess between the pews from food, drinks, newspapers, even alcohol bottles. People who have grown up in church know better than to litter the sanctuary in this manner; most unchurched people, on the other hand, don't see the difference between a sanctuary and a football stadium—we were getting a secular crowd. Each night as we vacuumed and scrubbed and filled trash bags, we praised God that we were attracting people who had perhaps never been to church before.

We were also attracting people from all over California, three and four hours away, coming in buses and caravans. We believed they shouldn't have to drive all that way only to find there was no more room. In fact many out-of-town groups called us before they came; to accommodate them we counted the exact number of people who were driving in from long distances and then reserved that many seats.

It was one of the most difficult things we did—holding empty seats until a group came while many in the audience were unable to bring in their extra family and friends. But such a practice really allowed the drama to touch a greater number of people in a greater area than just the city of Modesto. We realized that our community didn't have a monopoly on lost and hurting. If people who had never been to church before were willing to come great distances, we were willing to extend the courtesy of having seating for them; it may have made the difference in their lives.

Many, many young people from the community were coming as well. Our city, like most in America, had seen a rise in gang activity and youth criminality. Perhaps we had even experienced it with a little more force since we are located in California where ethnic groups from many countries come together and live right next to one another.

Gang members also continued to turn in their colors for the flag of freedom in Jesus; as the drama continued, I began receiving red and blue bandannas by the handful. They gave up their weapons too; I collected a number of sinister-looking knives—switchblades, hunting knives, black knives, brown knives, thin-bladed knives, thick-bladed knives—instruments of destruction given up in an act of surrender and deliverance. I received drugs and drug paraphernalia, including baggies of cocaine, a needle, and cigarette lighters. These youth were literally giving up their satanic addictions right there at the altar. I put all the rags, the knives, and the drugs in a bag and called it my "bag of rags," and every night I held it up as a visual testimony of how hardened gang members and drug users were coming to the Lord. The impact of that demonstration was so powerful that other young people followed suit.

We were making ripples in the community's business and civic climate, not only by attracting out-of-towners—who, after all, spent money on hotels and gas and food—but by causing daily traffic jams at the intersection of Coffee and Briggsmore. One Eye-in-the-Sky traffic station reported that there had been an automobile accident, which is what it looked like with all the cars stacked up on Coffee Road. Eventually, someone told them about "Heaven's Gates," at which time they reported it to their listeners, giving us some free publicity. But the cars kept coming, so many that the city had to send down the police to direct traffic along Coffee Road. It was not long before we got a call from some of the local restaurants wanting to know which nights the drama would be taking place so that they could bring on extra staff to handle the crowds overwhelming their establishments. That was not including, of course, the people who, when the weather let up a bit, brought their RVs and trucks and barbecues and hosted tailgate get-togethers in our parking lot.

Within a week of our first presentation, the local media came knocking on our office doors. They sniffed a story in our crowded church and wanted to know exactly what was going on—why people were crowding into a church rather than a dance club or a pool hall. The first headline, only six days after that first Sunday, read "Religious drama a hit: Throngs fill Calvary Temple nightly." "Modesto may not have seen this kind of sustained religious fervor since Billy Graham's crusade in 1948," the journalist wrote. "At least three times, more than one thousand people have been turned away. . . . The seats are not just packed with repeat spectators from the amen corner, either. . . ." The story made the front page of the religion section, complete with a full-color photograph of the actor playing Jesus welcoming people into heaven, surrounded by angels on the golden steps leading to the pearly gates.

If people had not heard of "Heaven's Gates" by then, they certainly would over the next couple of weeks; as the drama got bigger and bigger, news crews came from farther away to get a story.

One Sacramento television station came to do a live interview in the lobby of the church just before the performance. In the glare of the lights, with the microphone in my face, I was able to tell people all over Central Valley that the reason people were coming to our church was because we were giving them something that was in short supply most everywhere else: hope.

I began appearing on the local Christian television station with weekly updates about the revival, and the influence of those broadcasts was widely felt.

Then the newspaper ran a photograph of a policeman in the pouring rain directing traffic near our church: Behind him was a line of cars, their headlights on, going back as far as the eye could see.

Not long after that the newspaper would run a banner headline, declaring "REVIVAL" over a picture of our sanctuary, which looked like a sea of people gathered around the stage. "Modesto has probably never witnessed a religious event that caused a greater stir than 'Heaven's Gates,'" said the accompanying article, comparing our production again to the great Billy Graham crusade of 1948 (during which, incidentally, Graham and others with him produced "The Modesto Manifesto," a document setting guidelines of moral purity for members of his evangelistic team, a document that became a model for other evangelical ministries as well).

But after two weeks, we began to feel the cost of revival. It was costing us family time, sleep, and virtually everything else in our lives. There is a cost to anything worth having, and the greater the worth, the greater the cost. The only time faith does not cost is when it is dead, and the only time when church requires nothing of its members is when it is dead too. I was learning that true revival takes away normal routine, discards prearranged schedules, and throws everyone into an entirely new circumstance.

We had been putting on the performance every night at the cost of every other activity our church normally conducted: Wednesday night meetings were off, as were the youth get-togethers and Sunday evening services. All had temporarily disappeared. We still had Sunday morning services, but they were largely centered around the revival. Church regularity, an important component in retaining new believers I felt, had basically gone out the window. Without a regular church schedule I knew it would be difficult to bring people into the fold and get them involved.

If we had just been having an in-house move of God, where Christians were being blessed, that would have been a different story; if we had been having healing services or signs and wonders, that would have been different too, because you don't need to follow up with those people. They are already in the church; they are already saved and going to heaven.

But new believers are different altogether in that they desperately need Christian contact. They are like newborns, needing to be taken care of by Christian "grown-ups" otherwise, like the seeds in the Parable of the Sower, their new faith would be choked out by worldly concerns, and the new life would die.

Not only that, but our drama participants, particularly the actors and actresses, were exhausted by the end of the second week, physically unable to keep up with a nightly schedule. None of them had planned on going more than three nights—they had not seen any reason to ask their bosses for a vacation or their spouses for a "leave of absence." When the adrenaline rush of revival begins to drop off, the available human energy does too, and people begin drawing on their own reservoirs of emotional, physical, and spiritual strength to complete the task. Human energy is limited, and God's blessings, when they are plentiful enough, can wear us out. God is limitless, but people are not. God is infinite, we are but a vapor. God is eternal, we are but earthen vessels—nothing more than mud, fashioned to hold just a part of His life-energy.

I know that in every football game I ever played, the offense at some point had to take a rest, either by punting or by taking a time out, and there were even breaks built into the game (halftime, for example) so that the players wouldn't drop dead on the playing field. Just as the physical body can break down, so can the spiritual body of the church if it is not given time to rest.

I was most concerned because when people are being taxed beyond their limits day after day they get burned out, and there is a danger that negativity will set in.

I didn't want our follow-up callers to get cynical about the new Christians they were contacting and begin treating them with indifference. I didn't want the actors limping through their parts (there are no sagging angels in heaven). I didn't want our nursery workers to go crazy with other people's children. And I didn't want our parking attendants to lose their sunny demeanors. So we made the decision in one of our strategy meetings to start holding the drama three times on the weekend and not at all from Monday to Thursday in order to give ourselves time to follow up with the new believers, incorporate them into our church, and get them involved. We would take the rest of the week for ourselves so we could rebuild our health and energy and pour ourselves into each weekend's series of performances.

Considering all of the minute details that went into a successful performance, I continued to marvel at the fact that we were able to put on the drama three times a week. It would have been easy to get fascinated with the big picture, the vision and the grandiosity, but behind that a lot of work and a lot of little decisions kept the production going. Batteries, for instance: Every one of our many, many radios and flashlights had to have enough batteries to go through the night, and somebody had to go out and buy them. Ballpoint pens: We bought out the city, using every ballpoint pen they had for insertion in our salvation packets. Crackers for the nursery, air conditioning for the sanctuary, the upkeep of the stage and the costumes, the health of the actors, the extra trash cans needed for cleanup (which sometimes took all night)—all of these things took the time and effort of one or more people and could not be taken for granted lest the whole production grind to a halt.

We also had a major task in keeping up with the wear and tear of the facilities. Most churches aren't built to have three thousand people crammed into them night after night, especially when intended to seat only twenty-five hundred. We were stuffing more people into our pews than ever before, and the pews started to break. First they just began to crack and sag with the weight of hundreds of people over a period of hours, and then they shattered entirely right out the bottom. Each night this was a problem. To remedy the situation we had carpenters come after the performance and work into the wee hours, repairing the splintered pews and reinforcing others with supplemental bolts and planks. We had at least thirty pews break over the course of the drama.

The problem with the pews resulted from a decision we had made from the start: We wouldn't lock the doors even after the sanctuary was full. As Christians we wanted an open-door policy, because we never knew who would come through the door and find Jesus that night. We did print big signs that said Full and put them all over the sanctuary, but we simply wouldn't keep anyone out who wanted to come in and stand in the foyer and listen. We just required them to be a little more determined to get in.

Another major concern was the safety of everyone who attended, because if we had had one safety hazard, one accident, one mishap, it not only would have shut down the drama, it could have resulted in a lawsuit big enough to shut down the church.

Going to three nights a week allowed us to begin fortifying our church from the inside out, pulling people into service whose faith had been electrified by the drama.

Chapter **33**

Something No Minister Wants to Do

ost ministers don't ever face the problem of having to stop a move of God. I even hesitate to use that terminology because it's something no minister wants to do. We are supposed to encourage moves of God, not bring them to a halt. We are supposed to call on the Spirit to visit us, not ask Him politely to leave. But, as I was soon to find out, there is very little literature or scholarly writing on how to bring a successful revival to a close. There are few, if any, Bible college courses on how to slow down a tremendous move of the Spirit. It's not something we as preachers prepare for because we are more concerned about getting God to move in the first place. There is plenty of literature on preparing for revival, but hardly any on how to deal with massive revival when it comes.

Revival changes the shape of your church in the way pregnancy changes the shape of a woman's body. But pregnancy is temporary. Eventually the body must return to its original shape, and the new life must be taken care of.

As a church, we were experiencing something akin to pregnancy, except that our entire church focus was external instead of internal. The community had given birth to new converts, and we were playing the role of the overworked midwife. In situations like that you begin to realize how much work you have put into the "inside" things and how much you have prepared for things outside of the church.

As ministers we spend years learning how to tend our church, handling the finances, the vision, the staffing, the maintenance, and so forth. But during the revival the focus was on the people outside the church, the new family members coming in. No amount of administrative skill was enough to prepare us for the seismic shift in priorities.

At the end of February, after the drama had been going for a month and a half, I felt it was time to bring it to a close.

I had several reasons. First, I felt in my spirit that this was intended to be a Great Commission revival, which meant that we had to "make disciples" of the people we had won to the Lord. I didn't want 5 or 10 percent retention, I wanted to retain every single person that had come forward to our altar. It didn't matter to me that we might keep going and have more people saved and be able to say, "Wow! Look at all the thousands more we saw saved by going a few extra weeks!" if in fact those people were not even going to church anymore. What is the use of soul-winning if it's not coupled equally with soul-growth? It would be like picking more boxes of peaches than you and your entire family could eat. The last thing you want to do is take so many that they begin to spoil, instead of leaving them on the tree so you could at least get them next time around.

I brought the question before my staff of ministers, and we all felt of the same mind. We hated to see it stop, but we knew, we had a peace in our hearts, that it was the right time. Man's way of telling when something should stop is by waiting until the numbers slow down. God knows when you have had enough, and He was telling us that it was time to stop. We held a matinee on that Sunday, which we had not done before (and that was packed out), and then we had our final performance that evening. The response that night was perhaps greater than any of the previous nights, and no part of the drama had diminished over time—not the enthusiasm, not the numbers, not the excitement, not the emotion.

After our final performance, David Ford gave the last altar call, and as people crowded the stage one more time, the curtain dropped on one of the most incredible visitations of God Modesto had ever seen.

Chapter **34**

Spiritual Aftershocks

he days and weeks after the drama were a time for normalizing, for coming back to a church routine, with one major exception: We had a very large number of new believers that needed to be brought into the day-to-day life of the church.

In a sense it was introduction time for both of us. They had never seen our church in a normal state. They had not seen me preach on an average Sunday. They had not been attending when revival was not happening, so we both were experiencing a little bit of edginess (just as there is when developing any new relationship).

Were they going to like it now that they were members? What would they think of our choir and our singing? Would they enjoy our Sunday school classes and our staff and our people? They liked the drama, but did they like us? These are all questions we ask when becoming part of a new family, because we are observing on a deeper level and really deciding whether or not to make that commitment.

Though the drama stopped, there were spiritual aftershocks. People were still being touched, people were still bringing their friends. We had to add another morning service to accommodate everyone who wanted to come. I felt like our church had taken three steps forward—very quickly! We seemed to experience a growth spurt: Our worship and our praise and our unity as a body began to flourish like never before. It made me realize that though I was the appointed leader of the church, our course was really being steered by Someone much greater than I, and I was, in many ways, along for the ride just like everybody else.

Soon, however, we had to get around to the matter of numbers. The media attention kept coming from national and international news media, and we had to get our facts together to present to them. People, particularly in the media, need numbers to help them understand the impact and importance of what has happened. When they report on disasters—earthquakes, plane crashes, automobile pileups—the first thing they do is number the dead, the injured, and the missing. When they report on politics or public opinion, the first resource they use to illustrate their point is the poll, which gives a nice, neat number.

I have never preached or evangelized with the purpose of scoring big with numbers. In fact, during the revival, I never sought out the media and never tried to make a big deal of what was happening, because that was not my heart. God knew what God did, and that was good enough; I didn't need to be a guest on any talk shows or write up press releases. But when something like this happens, word gets around, and pretty soon you can't avoid it.

People were curious about what went on. They wanted to know how many people came and how many were saved. They wanted to know what we did to get them to come. They wanted to know the "secret" of our success. Though we had not gone through the revival with those kinds of intentions, we felt the need to look back on what had happened and at least be able to give people on the outside some picture, some idea, of what we had experienced and what the outcome was.

I called a meeting with the staff and told them that we needed to look at the numbers involved in each night and in the revival as a whole. I told them we didn't want to just pick numbers out of the air, we wanted to base them on solid facts so that they accurately reflected the truth. I wouldn't tolerate hype, because when we hype the works of God for pride's sake, the work of God is hindered and diminished. If anything, I said, we wanted to shoot low so that we could stand by the figures and not have to make any excuses.

We knew that over eighty-one thousand people had attended because we had just under three thousand people in our sanctuary for twenty-nine performances. We had a number of ways of counting those who had come forward to the altar, and one way was by counting the number of salvation packets we had handed out. We knew how many packets we had handed out by the number of ballpoint pens and cards and other materials we had bought to put inside the packets. It was, perhaps, tedious calculating those things, but our staff stuck with it, and we began to come to an idea of how many people had come to our altar.

The woman from the local television station, who had done our camera work and who had had many years of experience determining crowd capacities, insisted that fifty thousand people had come forward over the course of the revival. I told her I was not going to use that figure because I didn't have any additional evidence to verify it. Many other people on our staff were certain that between thirty-five thousand and thirty-eight thousand were saved.

After talking with all the people who had been involved in putting together the packets, all those who had collected the cards from people who had been saved, all those who had made phone calls, and everyone else who had knowledge that could help us reach a conclusion, I decided on thirty-three thousand as a conservative estimate. There are a number of reasons that that figure should be higher, but in the end we felt safest going with a number nobody could dispute.

Unlike many other revivals, the Modesto revival did not simply run its course, until people stopped coming. Because we had chosen to stop it while it was still on the rise, an unexpected effect followed: Our people wanted more. They could taste the victory; they knew there was more grain to gather in the fields, more grapes in the vineyard, more fruit in the orchard. Instead of being burned out and developing a mind-set that said, *It happened once and we ran it into the ground; therefore, it will never happen again,* we did just the opposite. The people began to say, "It happened once and even then we did not get the full measure of it. We are still hungry for it, and we are believing for it to happen again and will not stop working and praying until it does."

The revival had warmed our hearts and souls—never again would we doubt what God could do. The reality had been seared into our memories; our eyes had been opened; we had seen for ourselves the awesome power of God at work in our own midst. We could never forget that. Our ministry to the city now had an anchor holding us fast to the promise of revival. We had a confidence and assurance and unity gained only by going through large battles and experiencing total victory together: We had seen it and we knew it could happen again. If God could save thirty-three thousand people using a drama about heaven and hell in a church located in an agricultural city during the space of forty-seven days and twenty-nine performances, He could do anything.

Many of my ministers came to me during the revival or soon after and confessed that they had heard what I had said about the city being won through outreach, but they had not really thought it would happen in as great a manner as it did. They were happy to say that I had been closer to the mark. But I could not take credit for what had happened, nor could I say that I had expected such an unbelievable move. God was right when He said in Habakkuk 1:5 that we would have to see some things to believe them. If He would have told me what was going to happen—that over thirty-three thousand people would be

163

saved at our drama presentation—I probably would have kept it quiet so people wouldn't have thought I was delusional.

We are told to preach on what we believe can happen, like the Ninevah story where six hundred thousand people were saved in one city. But no matter how many times that sermon is preached, the Lord still tells us that there are things that our minds cannot comprehend unless we see them. That is where I was, and so was everybody in our church, because even though we believed in the vision He had given us, there are some gifts the Lord has in store for us that we cannot imagine until we receive them.

The same was true of many people outside the church, people who never thought they would see a church body that actually had a pulse and would impact their community. There are certain words that pop into the mind of every nonbeliever when the word "church" is mentioned: *musty, dusty, dull, boring, dark, smelly, hymns, sermons, guilt, sin, discomfort, sleep*. Now the revival associated a whole new set of words with the word "church": *vibrant, new life, Spirit-filled, joyful, active, deliverance, forgiveness, music, packed out, anointed, unified.*

Chapter **35**

Not Just for Modesto

I n Modesto, the revival continues to this day. The pastors from all denominations who met and prayed together before the revival continue to press forward together for the cause of Christ. In the summer of 1996 we held an outdoor rally with the theme "Break Down the Walls"—nine thousand people from the city showed up in one-hundred-degree weather. The local newspaper was flabbergasted; they still didn't understand the power of the Spirit to move people to do unusual things.

We have run the "Heaven's Gates" drama twice since its original presentation and have seen more than thirteen thousand saved. It is impossible to find somebody in our town whose life or family or friends were not changed by the drama. I appear every Wednesday morning on a television show that goes throughout northern California, and I often have guests who were saved during the Modesto revival. Recently I hosted my neighbors who had been Catholics and then atheists before the Lord got hold of them.

There is, in point of fact, a revival of revival in the United States, and if you doubt that, just ask anyone from the many churches who are seeing God move in ways like never before in this generation. Up until this point, and all during the '70s and '80s, many books were written about "the coming revival in America," "how to prepare for revival," "the next wave of revival," and so on. Those authors and observers were well-informed. The age of revival is now upon us. We are entering into a new era of higher expectations for the people of God, more responsibility for the condition of our communities, the rise of evangelism and outreach, an awakening in the souls of the dead in our churches, and a desire that burns deep inside us to win the lost while there is still time.

Our church—Calvary Temple Assembly of God in Modesto, California—has been touched by the new wave of revival. We can testify to the outpouring of the Spirit we received as a result of God's grace and our obedience. We can testify to the fact that it is a Spirit-led phenomenon, not a man-made occurrence, and that it overwhelmed our staff and congregation and pushed us to use our energies in ways we would never have thought possible. We can testify to the fact that we were utterly astounded by what we saw and will never again doubt what God can do.

Unfortunately, many people in America don't know what revival is because they have no firsthand experience. This is true of the past several generations. In fact, revival has become so rare that most of us have not even noticed the absence of it, and, as a result, the definition has been distorted with time. One writer correctly characterized revival as "a prairie fire ignited by a bolt of lightning from heaven." But nowadays we confuse revivalism with in-church evangelism. We have redefined it to fit our current conceptions of the way God moves among us. We have changed the meaning so the word has lost its power. We may have a good meeting on Sunday evening in one of our churches, and we call it revival. We may get an emotional feeling during a sermon, and we call that revival too. We may have a crusade with a visiting evangelist that everyone in the church attends, and we see people getting the Holy Ghost shakes or doing a Pentecostal jig, and we call that revival. But we think that is as far as it goes.

The truth is that revival is so much more than that. True revival is never an in-church experience; it is never hemmed in by the exit doors of our sanctuaries. When revival hits, it hits a whole area, a whole region, a whole people, a whole nation. It is aimed at the entire human family, not just the members of one particular church. Churches do not experience revival—cities do, and communities, and countries. Revival is not a captive flame nor a domesticated pet. Revival is not our gift to God; it is God's gift to us. Revival knows no boundaries. It makes no distinctions of economic status or educational background or skin color or nationality or social group or personal history. When God speaks, He speaks to all of us, and the whole world must listen to what He has to say.

This book is about experiencing revival like we have not seen in decades. It's about seeing God build up a vision in the heart, watching that vision shatter, and then allowing God to rebuild the vision and restore the miracle. It's about servanthood and obedience in the church, about evangelism, about going out of our way as never before to save the sheep caught in the bush, the sheep stuck between the rocks, the one down in the ditch, the one with the broken leg or the torn and battered flesh, the one we find wandering and bleating in hopelessness and fear. This book is about how your city can experience revival when a church believes for it and what our church did when it came to Modesto. This book is the story behind the newspaper headline, the personal account behind the numbers, the testimony behind the triumph. It's the story of God's faithfulness and how the only cure for a broken dream is to dream again.

This book is merely a testimony, a written account of the Lord working in a miraculous way. It is, in a sense, a manual in story form. The stories are all true, the testimonies real, and the numbers represent real people, real changes, actual individuals who have found the light and will now join us in heaven when Christ establishes His kingdom.

Since the revival took place, our church has continued to grow and prosper in the Lord. We are entering into a building program that will greatly expand our facilities, adding a gymnasium, classrooms, places for social gatherings, weight rooms, music studios, and much more, for the purpose of giving people in the city a place to go that is wholesome and safe. My hope is that the church will become a landmark in the Central Valley, a beacon, a family gathering center, an all-purpose church that takes care of its people from Monday through Sunday. If you read the Bible you see that most social events took place at the temple, but nowadays we don't have that. Every other place in town has the fun stuff for youth and entertainment for parents. But we want to start showing the movies on Friday nights, having the ball games on the weekdays, baseball leagues in the spring, and so on. We have allowed the world to steal away our family time, splitting us up so that the youth go over here and the parents go over there, and no one is together anymore. We want to provide for the social needs of the church in a whole-person approach to ministry.

The people at Calvary Temple are behind the new program with their pocketbooks as well as their hearts. On one Sunday alone we raised 1.7 million dollars for our building program, and are well over 3 million for the entire project. We have a Christian elementary school. We are going to keep adding grades until we go through high school. We plan to offer the best academic program in the area, while also giving youth the crucial spiritual development many are lacking. We are going to continue building our Global Outreach Bible Institute for the training of leaders and missionaries, because that has always been a part of my vision for evangelism.

The purpose of having new buildings is to enlarge our capacity to bring people in as God keeps sending them our way. The miracle of revival is continuing in our midst. A spirit of evangelism has come to rest on our church, such that our regular services on Sundays, and particularly on Sunday nights, are no longer predictable. The Spirit has been moving so powerfully that I am convinced God sometimes wants me to sit down so He can preach!

In a recent Sunday night service, people started standing up— "Preacher, I am an alcoholic, and I want to be healed." "Pastor, I am fourteen years old and addicted to crank, and I want deliverance." "Pastor, I can't wait for the end of the service, I want to get saved now!"

Some services consist of nothing more—and nothing less—than praise and worship, where the people know that the sweet presence of the Lord is among them.

But I believe that this revival was not given to us as an isolated incident nor as something we ought to brag about or keep from others. When somebody has a light it is meant to illuminate the lives of others, to allow them to see and experience the same things. The Modesto revival was not meant just for Modesto, it was meant for every church in America, every city, every community.

Our church has become a spiritual emergency room for the breaking of bondages and chains in people's lives. Everyone knows where the nearest hospital in their town is because it might be a matter of physical life or death someday. But what people in Modesto are realizing is that their spiritual status is in chronic shape even though they may feel physically healthy, and they are coming to our spiritual trauma center to get rid of their demonic oppressions, their addictions, their hurts, their angers. Nobody wants to go to a hospital where the paramedics don't know how to take care of injuries or to a facility that cannot take care of an infection. In the same way, who wants to go to a church where they are not treating people for their various bondages? Who wants to go where the preacher says, "Well, I don't know if we can help you with that area you are struggling with . . ." No! People go where the treatment is, and the treatment is always where the Holy Spirit is, where people don't inhibit His work with their unbelief or cast doubt on the promises of God.

It is probably no coincidence that our church is located right across the street from the biggest hospital in the area, with two helicopters and state-of-the-art equipment. The Spirit has directed people from all over our city to come to our church to experience real power in their lives. We don't bog them down with all sorts of doctrinal things first—"Are you paying your tithe? Are you a member? Have you been baptized in water? Is your family saved? Do you come from a Christian home? Do you believe in the gifts of the Spirit?"—no, we deal with their problem first and then begin to train them in Christian living. You don't ask if a person is eating healthy until you have sewn up his wound.

Here is a powerful question that I present as a challenge to Christian leaders: How many of us really believe what we preach? "The Spirit will be poured out upon us in the last days," we say, but how many of us really think that is going to happen, and more importantly, how many of us are prepared for it when it does? How many pastors know how to handle an avalanche of people coming into their church? Where is the instruction booklet or leadership manual on that? If these are the last days, and we are preaching last days sermons and preaching that revival is going to become a normal occurrence— not just in the big-city tent crusades but in the local churches—how many local churches are really prepared? How many local churches are believing for revival in their cities? How many are prepared to see their church radically changed in constitution, purpose, and character?

These are critical questions for every leader in America, because revivals don't happen in a vacuum. They are not signs of God's favoritism. As much as I was blessed by our revival, it was not some sort of reward for my good deeds or a vindication of what we were doing at our church. Revival is intended for all churches. A revival like this one is God's way of setting up a new platform and giving us just a taste of what is to come as the last days continue. The church, your church and ours, can become the permanent home of those hard cases who are giving up old destructive lifestyles and taking on new ones; that, after all, is the purpose of the gospel.

But, unfortunately, people do not often think of church as a place for "bad people." They think of it as a place for perfect people, people with no problems, people with perfect teeth who never have to go to the dentist. Yet it's vital to maintain a right spirit among the believers in our churches toward the lost, to see them not for what they are, but for what they were intended to be. I remember a sermon I preached on a Sunday during the revival titled "The Greatest Story Jesus Ever Told." I wanted the people of the church not just to tolerate the lost, to share the pew with them, however generously, but to fully share the heart of God toward them. The sermon was based on the Parable of the Prodigal Son. I asked them to imagine the grace of the father who joyfully took his son back after the son had totally rejected him, had gone so far as to tell his father that he wanted his share of the inheritance, as if the father were already dead.

I used an illustration from parenting: We do everything for our children from the moment they are born, changing their diapers, feeding them, taking them to school, driving them places, sacrificing ourselves in every way and giving to them. And then one day we ask them to clean their rooms, and they turn on us with a sarcastic attitude and say, "Yes, Sir," and from that moment they begin to reject us. Every parent knows that nothing cuts deeper than the rejection of one's own child, because children have direct access to their parent's heart.

Yet our Heavenly Father never reacts as we sometimes wish we could: to slam the door in their face, to reject them as they have us, to want them to know how it hurts. That is because we lack grace, but if only we knew what a world not buffered by grace would be like, if only we knew how hard it would be to live graceless—how many jagged corners and rough spots would scrape and cut us each day— we would be on our knees every day thanking God that He has spared us such an existence and has granted us forgiveness.

We need to have the grace for others that God has for us. Too often the church takes on the character of the older brother: "I'm in church every day, I'm much better than those guys down at the bar or those who stay home. I deserve the In Church All the Time Award, and these good-for-nothings deserve the pigsty."

171

That is a hell-bound attitude. The Lord says that when the master found the lost sheep he called his neighbors to rejoice with him, and when the woman found her lost coin, she called her friends to rejoice with her. The God of heaven rejoices in the presence of His angels every time one person is saved. Think about that for a moment. Can you imagine God himself rejoicing? Kicking up His heels in celebration? Singing out of sheer happiness? Who are we to decide that we will not rejoice right along with Him? Who are we to stand in judgment of a person who finally comes to the light? As a church, we need open, unselective arms; we need to welcome the hurting, the outcast, those in the worst of situations. In fact, we need to ache for the lost like God does, because if we don't, we will never be effective soul winners.

If your church has an open spirit toward the lost, then, like ours, it will become a home for runaways, barflies, druggies, abusers, abused, walk-outs, divorcees, murderers, white supremacists, criminals, and drinkers—the kind of people Jesus was not afraid to dine with when He was on this earth. The church needs to become a place of refuge again in a sin-ravaged world.

Revival comes in many ways. In your church it may come suddenly during your normal routine; it may come with a guest speaker; it may come during the holiday season; it may come in the praise and worship during your services; or it may come with a drama.

We produced a video documentary of the Modesto revival that is continuing the work begun here in January 1995. It has been amazingly effective in portraying what happened at the corner of Coffee and Briggsmore and has already made its way around the country. I received a letter from a woman that included a school photograph of her daughter, a pink-cheeked, red-haired little girl named Michelle. The letter said, "Recently a dear friend of mine whose son died in an airplane accident lent me your video called 'Miracle in Modesto.' I was particularly touched by the drama because I too have a daughter in heaven. Our nine-year-old daughter, Michelle Marie, went home November 5, 1993, when struck by a car while she was attempting to reach her school bus stop. . . . I will enclose a copy of Michelle's picture taken fifteen days before she went home . . ."

The news reports and word-of-mouth accounts also continue to bring this revival to world attention. A recently saved criminal judge from Modesto went to the Holy Land and a pastor from England, coming out of the Lord's tomb, heard he was from Modesto. He responded with excitement, saying to him, "Isn't that where that great revival took place?" Upon learning that the judge was not only from the city but had attended the very church he was asking about, the pastor was nearly knocked off of his feet with excitement.

Many other churches across American and Europe have hosted "Heaven's Gates & Hell's Flames" since we hosted it, and many are seeing dramatic results just as we did. But for Debbie and me the revival held especially important meaning in the context of what we had been through in our lives. It was a rebirth, a calling back to the great things of God. What God had said years earlier—"He has hedged me before and behind"—were true. The miracle of revival had been woven into the larger tapestry of our lives, confirming God's faithfulness to us, proving that no one's life is ever wasted and that temporary brokenness is actually a drawbridge that leads to greater lands and greater victories.

Epilogue

*T*he people whose testimonies I told you earlier are all doing well and are wonderful examples of new life transformation.

TAMMY JONES, THE MOTHER WHO LOST HER CHILDREN and was on drugs for many years, attends our morning services and volunteers in the preschool nursery. Her son, Earl, is a straight-A student in junior high, and Tammy gave birth to another child. She wants everyone to know how happy she is about the change God has made in her life and that His mercies are new every morning to anyone who will claim them.

JAVIER MACIAS, THE YOUNG BOY FROM GUATEMALA, is now a bright, cool-mannered sixteen-year-old who loves to talk, and when he talks it's usually about church or God or his personal testimony. Just ask his friends, his teachers, or his aunt; they have all heard about it plenty of times. They have also noticed the change in Javier's life, in fact, many of them were shocked by it.

"You hear what happened to Javier?" whisper students in the hallway. "Yeah, he's not the same guy!"

Javier is always eager to tell others about how he found the Lord, how his life has been totally transformed.

Javier is at our church so many times a week it has almost become his second home. Every Sunday morning I see him walking from his Sunday school class into the sanctuary, carrying his leather-bound Bible and talking theology with one of his classmates. He recently played a part in a youth drama we had during the Halloween season in which five hundred youth were saved. Javier still wants to be an evangelist.

AFTER FORTY-SIX YEARS OF HATRED, VIOLENCE, guns, and bar fights, the transformation of Doug Adams was going to take time. He began ushering with us, but he continued to carry knives, wore his hair down his back and his beard to his chest, wore all-black clothing, including a black cowboy hat worn low just above his eyes, smoked cigarettes, and cussed the proverbial blue streak. Like the rest of us, he had felt the Spirit in Modesto, and from the moment he accepted it he never looked back to the old ways. He devoted himself to church work, and slowly the transformation of Doug Adams began to take place before our very eyes. Week after week his beard and handlebar mustache got shorter and shorter. He began giving up his knives, one by one. Then he gave up smoking, bought white clothes instead of black, and turned in his cowboy hat and his Klan robes to me as an act of separation from his old life. He still wore his dog tags around his neck, but embossed in the metal plates was the word *Forgiven.* Doug had so many doors that were closed in his life: his days in the war, his being sexually molested by a foster father, his days with the Klan. Cautiously and carefully he began opening them, allowing the light of truth to be shed on his experiences, cleansing himself of the hatred he had stored up like old furniture in an attic.

Within a few months he had fallen in love with a beautiful lady in our church, and they were married in the very restaurant where he had spent the last of his forty-six years of sin-filled living (the bar was closed after too many of the patrons were converted, and they used the restaurant for church banquets).

The drama brought Doug into service with us; it solidified his spirit and brought him closer to God. Doug is now an usher in our church,

175

a faithful giver to our building program, and a man who loves the Lord. In similar but less dramatic ways, the drama did that for everyone. For those who were on the fence or halfhearted, it brought a spirit of commitment to the Lord's work, a readiness to volunteer for anything. The drama brought excitement and more than enough Spirit work for every person. We realized that our church had been a standing army from the beginning, but we had needed the battle cry to rally the troops into action.

FRANK TANNER HAS STAYED WITH THE CHURCH as an enthusiastic member, even through his legal problems. He and many of the other people whose testimonies I shared are the success stories of this revival.

People often wonder if revival has a lasting impact on a city, and I can say—with the weight of proof solidly behind me—yes! Revival is not revival if individual lives are not transformed forever. In Modesto, that is exactly what happened and what is happening to this day.